THE CLEAN HOME

THE CLEAN HOME

EASY-TO-FOLLOW TIPS AND SIMPLE ROUTINES TO CREATE
A CALM, CLEAN HOME YOU CAN ENJOY EVERY DAY

KATRINA SPRINGER

THE ORGANISED HOUSEWIFE

MACMILLAN
Pan Macmillan Australia

Dedication

For my kids, Joshua, Isabella and Haylee.

And my husband Scott, who has always been a constant support, and without whom this book probably would not have happened.

CONTENTS

MY STORY

I'll begin with a confession: I haven't always been organised.

My home always had clutter spots (the dining table was my preferred dumping ground) and I struggled to keep the kitchen clean. I used every pot and utensil when I cooked and usually left the dirty dishes for the following day – relaxing seemed much more enticing than cleaning.

But when my husband and I welcomed our twin babies in 2003, followed by our youngest daughter just two years later, I realised that I needed to make some changes. I soon discovered that cleaning routines helped to create calm among the chaos – and gave me more space and time to enjoy family life.

Growing up, I idolised my nan. With seven children (including twins) and 19 grandchildren, she was generous, capable and a proud homemaker. She delighted in keeping a neat, tidy and clean home, and she always had home-made baking waiting for us when we visited. I spent my school holidays with her, crafting, cooking and helping her with housework. I wanted to be just like her. (That said, I rarely kept my room tidy at home – I was always getting into trouble for kicking my dirty clothes under the bed!)

Sadly, Nan passed away a year after I got married. Later, when my twins were born, I missed her more than ever – I had so many questions I wanted to ask her. I am sure she would have given me some excellent heartfelt advice about raising a family and keeping a happy home.

Like her mother, my mum was also caring and nurturing, and proud of her home. She was a very organised hoarder and collector, and kept many gorgeous ornaments in a glass cabinet. My memories of her cleaning the house are as clear as yesterday. When Mum cleaned, she meant business. She removed everything from the cupboards, scrubbed from top to bottom, sorted through her things (rarely purging anything), then reorganised as necessary and placed everything back neatly. Mum repurposed old ice-cream containers and fruit boxes to keep everything in their place – I know she would have had a field day with all the items we stock at Organised HQ!

These two kind and capable women were a huge influence on me: Nan with her joy of baking and being surrounded by family; Mum, with her organisation and love of helping others.

I married my soulmate Scott when I was 21, and a few months later we purchased our first home here on the Gold Coast, Queensland. We shared our domestic responsibilities. I inherited my nan's love of baking and enjoyed cooking delicious muffins and biscuits for Scotty's lunch box. I did, however, struggle with keeping everything tidy. I am a messy cook and like to use every saucepan in the kitchen (this hasn't changed, I am still the same in this regard). I often left the dinner dishes for the next day – which I always regretted when I came home from work to a dirty sink. The dining table, especially, was my downfall. I would come home and dump the mail, my handbag, lunch bag, shopping – everything! – on the table, and there it would stay until our weekly cleaning afternoon.

Then, at the age of 25, I fell pregnant with twins. For health reasons, I had to stop work in my first trimester. Homebound, I spent months 'nesting', organising all the drawers, planning the twins' nursery, making sure everything was as orderly and simple as possible for their arrival. I was in my element, thoroughly enjoying the experience of creating a clean, organised home.

When our two bundles of absolute sweetness (a girl and a boy) arrived, life – and our home – was turned upside down. Two newborns take up a lot of time. Feeding alone could take a good hour and a half. Then there was the bathing, cuddling, playing, endless settling …

The domestic duties took second place. Loads of washing started to pile up; there was no time to fold the clean clothes. The dishes collected in the sink; I was always too tired to sweep the floors. Clutter crowded every surface.

I put on a happy face but deep down I was quietly overwhelmed by how disorganised everything had become. I didn't want to feel like this; it was interfering with my sense of wellbeing. I knew that in order to find some calm among all this chaos, I needed to create some routines. Our previous approach of tackling everything in one morning or afternoon was no longer achievable, so I split up the things I needed to do and dedicated specific days to certain tasks.

Monday	Grocery shopping
Tuesday	Bathroom/general tidy
Wednesday	Floors
Thursday	Bedrooms
Friday	Kitchen
Weekend	Various household tasks

Splitting the workload over specific days meant I could get the jobs done around the home when the twins were sleeping or happily playing. I quickly discovered that routines create structure, which then becomes habit, which automatically puts you in control of the day. Completing tasks that take just a couple of minutes can put you in a positive mindset for the rest of the day. So from that day forward, I have kept to a routine.

Two years later, we welcomed our youngest daughter and moved into a new home with room for our growing family. It was a struggle in the early days, but I had a good sleeping, feeding and play routine for the twins, and I managed to work my new baby into the established routine.

Of course I had many days when the washing was piling up (both clean and dirty), I didn't have the energy to tidy the house, and the kids just drove me crazy. Being a stay-at-home mum sometimes felt just like groundhog day. I'm not ashamed to admit that I would often put the kids in front of the television and have a little cry in my bedroom.

Three kids under three didn't leave much time for a lot, but the routines helped to keep my sanity intact. I found that my emotions were all over the place when the house was a mess, but when our home was tidy, I was much calmer. I also realised that I felt happy enough when the home was tidy and semi-clean; perfectly clean was impossible at that stage of my life. It was – and still is – all about balance and routine. I was beginning to work out what helped my mood and wellbeing, and learning to embrace imperfectly perfect standards (I write more about this on page 11).

For example, I realised that waking up to a dirty kitchen made me cranky – and that was a terrible way to start the day. Knowing this, I made sure that I cleaned the kitchen before bed, and this always took priority over other tasks, such as folding the clean washing. With these compromises in place, I found my happy spot.

Accepting that imperfectly perfect was good enough allowed me to be more productive, spend more time with the family and, importantly, look after myself. We all get so busy, and a lot of the time we put everyone else before ourselves. But self-care, be it a walk alone, a new haircut or keeping on top of medical checks, is absolutely vital. Please do not put your health at the bottom of the list. Being imperfectly perfect gives you more time to check in with yourself.

Routines, compromises and self-care all helped to create a happy, clean and calm home when the kids were little. When our youngest daughter started school, I spent some time reflecting on the early days of motherhood and I thought of the conversations I'd had at mothers' group. I remember asking the other parents things like, 'How do you keep on top of your washing?' and 'Do you have any good recipes? I'm stuck in a rut.' I was reaching out to see if other mums had the same issues as me – and if they had any solutions. Sadly, no one admitted they might be struggling on this front too, which at the time made me feel like I was doing something wrong. One on one, we would talk about our troubles, but not in a group setting. It was like no one wanted to admit openly that they needed a bit of help.

I realised that many women compare themselves to others. In fact, it's very hard not to. Others can seem to have perfect lives, lovely homes and no worries in the world. But the reality is that it's so easy to hide behind a smile and appear happy on the outside, when actually you might feel overwhelmed or unhappy.

It was then that I came up with the idea of creating an online forum where I could share my story and my tips and tricks for keeping a happy home. A friend helped me come up with the name. She said she had always considered me to be an organised housewife (mostly based on my very tidy fridge).

So in 2010, The Organised Housewife was born. I began typing up blog posts about how I meal planned and prepped, how I organised the fridge, my favourite recipes and the routines that helped me maintain my sanity. These everyday tips really resonated with people, and readers told me how they'd adapted my ideas to suit their own home and family. This inspired me to write more and share more, and in turn our online community just kept growing.

A couple of years after I started my blog, Mum passed away suddenly. It was a huge shock. The upkeep of the large family home with 12 acres became too much for my dad and he decided to sell. He, my brothers and I took nearly six months to go through everything that Mum collected in her lifetime, selling items or donating them to charity, or sometimes throwing them out. It was emotionally draining and I found myself exhausted and lonely with no desire to keep up with my own housework. This experience made me even more deter-mined to help those who feel overwhelmed by clutter. I realised the importance of taking it step by step, day by day, and that small changes add up to creating a home you love.

Never in my wildest dreams did I imagine that what I share would turn into what it is today: two businesses, the blog, The Organised Housewife, and the online store, Organised HQ. I now have wonderful team members who help support my dream and goals (and, boy, have they been amazing while I took time out to write this book). In fact, my team members created the word 'Katify' for me:

to describe not only the way I clean and organise (and my love of spread-sheets!), but more than that, how I reassure people that having a clean and tidy home is achievable – and that imperfectly perfect is perfectly acceptable.

And while I'm the first to admit I love a checklist, planner or storage container to help bring even more calm and organisation into the home, I also know that every home and every family is unique and there's no one-size-fits-all approach. All my tips can easily be adapted to suit your individual needs and circumstances. My aim is to inspire you, my readers, to find simplicity and joy in your home, whatever that might mean to you.

I often look back to my early years – how much I idolised my nan – and I feel very lucky to be doing my dream job. I do feel very thankful that I have been able to spend all these years doing what I do and helping others enjoy their homes. I am so proud of my family. I adore my children and have the most supportive husband who I know loves me unconditionally.

I hope this book helps you to:

Find balance

Create routines

Lower your expectations

Ask for help

Make your health a priority

Believe in yourself

Enjoy your home

And embrace the imperfect.

Kat xxx

Part 1

KEEPING A CLEAN HOME

The clutter in our lives, homes and heads can harm our happiness and our ability to focus and relax. Keeping a clean home can help to improve our mental and physical wellbeing by reducing stress, increasing productivity and maintaining good health.

The benefits of a clean home

Keeping a home clean and tidy can feel overwhelming at first, especially if you have young kids to look after and/or a busy full-time job. But taking the time to clean your home can help to enhance mental clarity and eliminate stress and chaos. It also saves you time, because you can quickly locate items, and money, because you are less likely to require repairs or replace furnishings and appliances.

Waking up to a clean home is always a great start to the day. I feel like once I make my bed each morning, I am already productive. It's such an easy task but it really does set the tone for the hours ahead.

The short time I spend investing in cleaning allows me to fully enjoy my home the rest of the time. It also gives me a sense of pride and accomplishment.

Other benefits of keeping a clean home include:

Eased allergies

Reduced safety hazards

Enhanced productivity

Improved sleep patterns

Increased physical movement.

WHAT IS CLEAN?

Everyone's definition of clean is different. Clean to one person may mean not a speck of dust in the home and everything is in its place; clean to another person could simply be a tidy home with some dust, or a clean bathroom and kitchen but toys scattered on the floor.

My definition of clean is that all the most-used spaces (toilets, bathroom and kitchen) are clean for hygiene purposes. While I tidy dishes at the beginning of the day and clean them at the end, I will usually always find dust laying around my home. I find that I don't have enough time for spotlessness – this is my imperfectly perfect version of clean.

EMBRACE THE IMPERFECTLY PERFECT

Let's be honest: when it comes to cleaning, perfection is not always achievable. You may not have the time, knowhow, finances or motivation – and that is perfectly human! Imperfection is real, especially in a home shared with children and pets. Rather than feeling overwhelmed or disheartened, I urge you to embrace the imperfect.

Putting pressure on yourself to be perfect or do a perfect job is setting yourself up for failure. When you don't reach the desired result because you've set your standards so high, you'll stop trying and feel overwhelmed instead. The goal is to just do it the best way you can.

Allowing yourself to accept imperfection as perfection will help you to reach your goals faster and feel proud of what you do achieve, as well as setting the path for future success.

We all have different home lives and we all have different standards. There is no point in comparing yourself to others. My friends and I do things differently, embracing the imperfectly perfect concept in our own way. For example, I only iron school uniforms and some tops and dresses. I don't iron linens, such as tablecloths, tea towels or pants. Sometimes I choose not to buy particular clothes as I think of my future self and the ironing that is involved. But one of my best friends, Anneliese, finds joy in ironing everything – to her, it's therapeutic. And while I know many prefer to iron sheets and pillowcases, I am happy to put wrinkled sheets on my bed as long as they are fresh and clean.

Similarly, neither my friend Alyce nor I turn family members' socks in the right way when washing or folding, and I never pair socks or fold underwear. Instead, I buy one brand of socks so they all look the same, sort socks and underwear into piles after they are cleaned, and place the pile into appropriately labelled tubs. But others like to pair socks and fold delicates neatly away into a drawer, not minding the extra time it takes as it makes them happy.

It all comes down to personal preference. I probably don't dust as often as I should, but I do make an effort to keep the floors clean. I wash my bed linen weekly because I like sleeping in clean sheets, but from a young age I got the kids to make their own beds each day, put away their clean washing and organise their drawers, despite the results making my eye twitch.

Be realistic with the time that you have to spend cleaning your home. You may realise you don't have a lot of extra time and that your standard of clean can be imperfectly perfect to match the time you have to complete the tasks.

Another tip: rather than completing all tasks in one go, you can use pockets of time throughout the day to tick off a few tasks from your list. If you find you are always trying to make the end result perfect, set a timer to limit yourself and learn that what you managed to do in the time you have is 'good enough'. If you can't finish it all, that's okay! You can finish it next time. You have at least started.

So please remember that imperfect can be perfect. This book is just a guide and you can follow the steps according to your own preferences and the time you have available.

My motto is:
Imperfectly
perfect is
good enough.

Kat's 7 Steps To Cleaning

1   Build a cleaning kit

(See page 45.) Make it easy for yourself by having your cleaning essentials on hand. Storing them in a portable caddy allows you to easily carry your kit around the house with you.

2   Create a cleaning routine

(See page 26.) A routine will help balance out all the areas that need cleaning throughout the home. Fitting cleaning into a busy schedule isn't easy. A routine will give you more freedom to enjoy your home and family without worrying that you should be cleaning. Seeing a list also allows you to delegate tasks to particular members of the household or to work out what you want to outsource.

3   Clean up sooner rather than later

Cleaning is always easier when it's done sooner. If a stain, for example, is on your carpet, it will be easier to get out now rather than allowing the stain to set in.

4 Follow instructions carefully

All cleaners, appliances, furniture, linens and clothes come with directions or care instructions that detail the best approach to clean and prevent damage. Always read instructions first.

5 Let the cleaning solution do the work

Many cleaning products require them to sit for a few minutes to be effective and break down the dirt and grime. To save you time, spray the cleaning product onto the surface and continue cleaning elsewhere. For example, spray the shower, then continue with other tasks in the room (cleaning the sink or emptying the rubbish) while the product is working its magic.

6 Learn Kat's Cleaning Cha Cha

Clean from top to bottom, left to right, back to front. This way, you won't miss anything or clean an area more than once, as it will prevent you from accidentally dropping dirt or dust onto a lower surface you have already cleaned.

7 Make it fun!

Put on your activewear and create a cleaning playlist filled with music that will energise you. I have one on Spotify: search 'The Organised Housewife Motivation Mix', do Kat's Cleaning Cha Cha (see above) and you'll blitz through the cleaning in no time!

GETTING EVERYONE INVOLVED

You don't have to do everything yourself. When it comes to family members or housemates, remember that it is their home as much as it is yours and everyone should be taking some form of responsibility to help keep it clean and tidy. Bear in mind that sometimes other family members, especially kids, can't see mess like you do. Sit down with your family and have a conversation with them. Try to keep the mood light, but let your feelings be known that you want and expect more help. Then stand back and let them have a go. Don't forget to encourage them by expressing thanks for their help.

ENCOURAGING KIDS TO HELP

I gave my kids responsibilities around the home at a young age and I am very appreciative of the contributions they make today. I created a routine chart when my kids first started school to help remind them of the tasks they needed to do. (This has become one of the most popular downloads at Organised HQ.) Children really are creatures of habit, so having an easy-to-see task chart or routine guide for them will make your home run a lot smoother and prevent you from repeating yourself every morning. My kids have become very respectful and I am extremely grateful that they are growing up to be such considerate human beings. If they see me at the washing line or folding laundry, they will come and help. In particular, my son usually does tasks he can see need doing, just before he sits down for a marathon session of gaming.

There are many benefits to encouraging the kids to help out around the house. Here are just a few reasons why you should get them involved:

Teaches them life skills

I think this is one of the most important lessons. Without chores – or responsibility tasks – as I prefer to call them – my kids would have no idea how to keep a room tidy or how to clean up after themselves. Cleaning teaches them to become more self-reliant and makes their progression into adulthood easier.

The value of teamwork

When everyone is required to pitch in around the house, it teaches kids the real value of teamwork and working well with others. It shows them how to listen, follow instructions and be a team player.

Responsibility and discipline

By assigning kids a task and giving them a responsibility, they quickly learn a lot about following rules and taking ownership of certain jobs.

Respect and appreciation

If children are never exposed to how much work goes into keeping a clean and tidy home, they will never know how much you do for them. By giving them a few of the small tasks, they will grow to appreciate your hard work.

It keeps them occupied

When your kids are bored, anything (even chores) can seem entertaining. Don't set them too many chores so that they resent them, but give them a job every now and then to keep them busy. Put on music to make it fun!

Work ethic and habits

Creating a list of tasks that they are responsible for each week helps them to form good habits. Even implementing a pocket-money system will assist them in developing a good work ethic.

Self-confidence and purpose

Completing a chore gives children a boost of confidence and makes them feel more capable. They will enjoy making an important contribution to family life.

Kat's tip

My kids helped me to tidy up the toys from the moment they could crawl. We would sing our packing-up song (that we made up ourselves), which made it fun. Now they are older, if they do leave something around the house, I do not pick it up. I call for them to stop what they are doing, because that's annoying – I pick my timing well, like when they are relaxing – and get them to pick up the item they have left laying around. That annoying factor encourages them to do it next time without having to be prompted. Other times, if they are hanging around me, I just need to look them in the eye, then eyeball the item, and they know exactly what needs to be done!

TASKS FOR KIDS UNDER 5

○ Put dirty clothes into laundry

○ Help sort dirty washing into darks, colours and whites piles

○ Put salt and pepper on table

○ Help dust

○ Help feed the pet

○ Pick up toys

○ Make bed – remember it can be imperfectly perfect!

○ Tidy bedroom

○ Get the mail

○ Help wash the car

○ Help fold tea towels

TASKS FOR KIDS AGE 5–7

All of previous, plus:

○ Put dirty clothes into correct laundry sorting basket

○ Use a handheld stick vacuum to clean small floor areas

○ Unpack dishwasher

○ Feed the pet

○ Help put away groceries

○ Help fold washing

○ Dusting

○ Wipe bathroom sink

○ Set the table

○ Water plants

○ Clean inside of car

○ Sweep outside patio and driveway

○ Help pack lunch boxes

TASKS FOR KIDS AGE 8–10

All of previous, plus:

- Peg washing on the line
- Take washing off the line
- Fold washing and put away their own washing
- Put rubbish in the outside bin
- Take out the bin on collection day
- Tidy bathroom
- Help with cooking dinner
- Pull weeds from garden
- Run own shower or bath

TASKS FOR KIDS AGE 10 AND OLDER

All of previous, plus:

- Load and turn on washing machine
- Change sheets on bed
- Clean toilet
- Clean bathroom
- Clean mirrors
- Vacuum
- Cook simple meals
- Clean car
- Clean fridge
- Clean and declutter kitchen bench
- Wash the dishes
- Make and pack own lunches
- Clean pool
- Pick up pet poo in backyard
- Take pet for a walk
- Bake for lunch box
- Ironing

ASKING FOR HELP

It's not uncommon for one person in the household (more than likely you) to feel like all the housework is left to them. Sometimes those around you may not realise you are struggling. I know it takes a lot of effort to admit you need help, but as the saying goes, ask and you shall receive. I rarely asked my mum for help. I wanted to prove to her that I was capable, but mostly I was stubbornly waiting for her to offer help. Sadly, after she passed away, I learnt that all she wanted was her daughter to ask for help, and to need her. This broke my heart and I wish I could go back and change it. I believe there are lessons to learn in everything: this made me realise that there is no shame in asking for help. And sometimes, you are not only doing yourself a favour but somebody else too.

GETTING A CLEANER

Let's be clear. Getting a cleaner to help with weekly, seasonal or annual tasks is perfectly acceptable. You can also outsource jobs such as the ironing, gardening, pet grooming, window cleaning and general fixing around the house.

I know many people say they would feel like a failure if they got a cleaner, or that they are judged because they do. I absolutely disagree! Paying a professional, budget permitting, to do the cleaning every week, fortnight or season means that you can spend that time doing something that is higher on your priorities list, whether that is working, exercising, practising some self-care, or spending more hours with your loved ones. It's also really important to listen to your body: if cleaning the entire house leaves you feeling overwhelmed or in pain, it's time to get some help. In short, getting a cleaner can lead to a happier and healthier version of you.

Part 2

CLEANING CHECKLISTS

With a clear plan, some pockets of time each
day and checklists to follow, you can create a
calm and healthy home to enjoy every day.

Creating a cleaning routine

Cleaning the home and keeping on top of all the tasks can seem to be never-ending – unless you have a plan. It really helps to create a cleaning routine based around you, your family, your time and your home's needs.

Having a checklist of tasks to complete helps to take the thinking out of what to do next.

Cleaning routines can be:

> **Daily tasks –** to help you maintain a clean and tidy home.
>
> **Weekly tasks –** split up into manageable tasks, one area per week or all completed in one day.

Before having children, we lived in a smaller house and I used to complete my cleaning routine all on a Saturday morning. But once kids came into the equation and we moved to a bigger house, I found splitting the routine up into rooms on particular days was more manageable.

Not everyone's cleaning routines will be the same. A couple living in a one-bedroom apartment will be very different to a family of five in a large home. The key is to be realistic, making your routine as time-efficient as possible and ensuring that it meets your personal living standards and needs. There is no right or wrong way! It's all about making the routine work for you.

And please remember my imperfectly perfect motto (page 13). It's about making your home clean enough that you are happy with it, then you can enjoy your home and feel relaxed for the rest of the day.

Kat's tip

As we have pets, I need to regularly
clean my floors to pick up their fur.
I like deep cleaning the floors on a
Friday or Saturday, so they're clean
for the weekend. I then give them
a quick vacuum on Sunday evening
or Monday morning to pick up any
dirt that swept in from outside and
again during the week to pick up
pet fur and food crumbs.

DAILY TASKS

I do a few basic tasks every day. These are tasks that don't take too much time or effort, but completing them ensures that I wake up and spend my day with a better mindset. All these tasks have now become a habit and I have the routine down pat to swiftly get through it.

Morning

- Make bed
- Quick bathroom tidy up
- Spot clean bathroom sink
- Quick kitchen tidy up
- Quick clean kitchen benchtop
- Quick clean kitchen sink
- Quick floor clean in kitchen
- Quick floor clean in living room
- Dry a load of washing
- Quick clean washing machine

During the day

- Fold and put away washing
- Quick bedroom tidy up
- Quick living room tidy up

Evening

- Sort dirty clothes
- Put on a load of washing
- Quick tidy up in laundry
- Quick clean laundry sink
- Clean the dishes
- Quick kitchen tidy up
- Quick clean kitchen benchtop
- Quick clean stovetop
- Spot clean oven
- Clean splashback
- Quick clean kitchen sink
- Quick clean kitchen sponge
- Quick bathroom tidy up
- Spot clean bathroom sink

Relax!

WEEKLY TASKS

Your weekly routine will be based on your family routine and the time you have available. For example, I like to clean bedrooms on a Monday as they're always a little messy after the weekend. I clean the laundry on Saturday, doing a few extra loads of washing to ensure school uniforms are ready. Sunday is usually a day off! I rest and relax, and spend it with family.

When creating your weekly routine, I suggest the following approach:

Create a task list – go through your home, separating room by room, writing down all the cleaning tasks you want to do.

Pick the best routine plan for you – decide if you want to do a little every day, one area each day of the week, or everything on the one day.

MONTHLY TASKS

These particular tasks, such as cleaning appliances, doors and windows, and deep cleaning bins, do not need to be completed as frequently. It's a good idea to tackle them each month to remove dust and dirt build-up, and keep appliances in good working order.

SEASONAL TASKS

These tasks will enhance the overall cleanliness of your home and ensure no corner or crevice is neglected.

ANNUAL TASKS

There are particular cleaning tasks that only need to be done once a year. These tasks can be spread out through the year.

KAT'S ROUTINE BY ROOM

These checklists are split into two different types of lists: a regular routine cleaning checklist and a deep cleaning checklist. Use the deep cleaning checklist if you want to blitz through a whole room clean in one go. It follows my Cleaning Cha Cha from top to bottom.

Living Area Cleaning Checklist

One of the most frequented rooms in the home, the lounge room is a place for the family to come together, to relax and play. Create that cosy feeling with clean upholstery, linens and appliances, ready for you to enjoy family time.

Daily

- ○ Quick tidy up
- ○ Quick floor clean

Weekly

- ○ Tidy, pick up and put away clutter
- ○ Dust light fittings
- ○ Quick clean curtains
- ○ Spot clean internal windows
- ○ Clean light switches
- ○ Clean door handles
- ○ Clean mirrors
- ○ Clean TV
- ○ Clean remote controls and electronic game controllers
- ○ Clean electronic devices
- ○ Dust ornaments
- ○ Dust and clean all surfaces
- ○ Quick clean lounge
- ○ Water plants
- ○ Clean floor

Monthly

- ○ Clean ceiling cornices
- ○ Dust top of door frames
- ○ Clean blinds/shutters
- ○ Quick clean internal windows
- ○ Clean windowsills
- ○ Clean throw blankets

Seasonally

- ○ Clean cushions
- ○ Clean light fittings
- ○ Clean ceiling fan
- ○ Clean air-conditioning filter
- ○ Clean walls
- ○ Dust wall hangings
- ○ Clean window tracks
- ○ Dust plants
- ○ Clean lounge
- ○ Clean skirting boards
- ○ Freshen up carpet

Annually

- ○ Deep clean curtains
- ○ Deep clean internal windows
- ○ Clean external windows
- ○ Deep clean rugs
- ○ Deep clean carpets

Living Area Deep Cleaning Checklist

Pick up
- ○ Tidy, pick up and put away all clutter

Wash
- ○ Cushions
- ○ Throw blankets

Clean
- ○ Light fittings
- ○ Ceiling cornices
- ○ Ceiling fan
- ○ Air-conditioning filter
- ○ Top of door frames
- ○ Walls
- ○ Wall hangings
- ○ Blinds/shutters
- ○ Curtains
- ○ Windows
- ○ Windowsills and tracks
- ○ Plants
- ○ Light switches
- ○ Door handles
- ○ Mirrors
- ○ TV
- ○ Remote controls and electronic game controllers
- ○ Electronic devices
- ○ All surfaces
- ○ Ornaments
- ○ Photo frames
- ○ Lounge
- ○ Skirting boards
- ○ Carpet
- ○ Rugs
- ○ Floor
- ○ External windows

Finishing touches
- ○ Put cushion covers back onto cushions
- ○ Spray with room spray

Kitchen Cleaning Checklist

Keeping the kitchen tidy through the day and at the end of the night will make it easier for you to relax. Plus, having a tidy kitchen makes cooking and baking much more enjoyable.

Daily

- ◯ Clean dishes
- ◯ Quick tidy up
- ◯ Quick clean benchtop
- ◯ Quick clean stovetop
- ◯ Quick clean splashback
- ◯ Spot clean oven
- ◯ Quick clean sink
- ◯ Quick clean kitchen sponge
- ◯ Quick floor clean

Weekly

- ◯ Tidy, pick up and put away clutter
- ◯ Deep clean linens and sponges
- ◯ Dust light fittings
- ◯ Quick clean curtains
- ◯ Dust and clean all surfaces
- ◯ Spot clean internal windows
- ◯ Clean light switches
- ◯ Clean door handles
- ◯ Quick clean pantry
- ◯ Quick clean fridge
- ◯ Quick clean microwave
- ◯ Quick clean rangehood

- ◯ Quick clean oven
- ◯ Quick clean appliances
- ◯ Quick clean dishwasher
- ◯ Quick clean cabinets
- ◯ Deep clean benchtop
- ◯ Quick clean bin
- ◯ Deep clean sink
- ◯ Clean floor

Monthly

- ◯ Clean ceiling cornices
- ◯ Dust top of door frames
- ◯ Clean blinds/shutters
- ◯ Quick clean internal windows
- ◯ Clean windowsills
- ◯ Deep clean sink drains
- ◯ Deep clean dishwasher
- ◯ Clean microwave
- ◯ Clean rangehood
- ◯ Clean stovetop
- ◯ Clean kettle
- ◯ Deep clean bin

Seasonally

- ◯ Deep clean oven
- ◯ Clean light fittings
- ◯ Deep clean top of cabinets
- ◯ Clean walls
- ◯ Dust wall hangings
- ◯ Clean window tracks
- ◯ Dust plants
- ◯ Clean skirting boards
- ◯ Deep clean pantry
- ◯ Deep clean fridge

Annually

- ◯ Clean behind fridge
- ◯ Deep clean curtains
- ◯ Deep clean internal windows
- ◯ Clean external windows

Kitchen Deep Cleaning Checklist

Head start

- ◯ Clean and put away dirty dishes
- ◯ Soak oven shelves
- ◯ Run oven self-cleaning function (If applicable)
- ◯ Start cleaning kettle
- ◯ Start cleaning microwave
- ◯ Start cleaning dishwasher
- ◯ Fill sink up with warm water and dishwashing liquid

Pick up

- ◯ Tidy, pick up and put away clutter

Wash

- ◯ Tea towels
- ◯ Kitchen sponges

Clean

- ◯ Light fittings
- ◯ Ceiling cornices
- ◯ Door frames
- ◯ Top of cabinets
- ◯ Walls
- ◯ Wall hangings
- ◯ Blinds/shutters
- ◯ Curtains
- ◯ Windows
- ◯ Windowsills and tracks
- ◯ Plants
- ◯ Light switches
- ◯ Door handles
- ◯ Kettle
- ◯ Microwave
- ◯ Inside of fridge
- ◯ Outside of fridge
- ◯ Pantry
- ◯ Rangehood
- ◯ Stovetop
- ◯ Oven
- ◯ Dishwasher
- ◯ Appliances
- ◯ Inside of cupboards
- ◯ Cabinets
- ◯ All kitchen surfaces
- ◯ Benchtops
- ◯ Splashback
- ◯ Bin
- ◯ Sink
- ◯ Skirting boards
- ◯ Floor

Finishing touches

- ◯ Restock supplies
- ◯ Add fresh clean linens
- ◯ Spray with room spray

Bathroom Cleaning Checklist

We use the bathroom to clean our bodies, so it's important to make sure we keep it hygienically clean for our own health too. A quick clean often will help to prevent mould and reduce scrubbing during the deep cleans.

Daily
- ○ Quick tidy up
- ○ Quick clean rubber bath toys
- ○ Spot clean sink

Weekly
- ○ Tidy, pick up and put away clutter
- ○ Wash bath towels
- ○ Wash hand towels
- ○ Wash bath mats
- ○ Wash face washers
- ○ Dust light fittings
- ○ Clean shower
- ○ Clean bathtub
- ○ Clean bath toys
- ○ Clean mirror
- ○ Clean soap dispenser
- ○ Clean toothbrush holder
- ○ Clean makeup brushes
- ○ Clean benchtop
- ○ Clean vanity cabinets
- ○ Clean light switches
- ○ Clean door handles

- ○ Quick clean rubbish bin
- ○ Clean toilet
- ○ Clean sink
- ○ Clean floor

Monthly
- ○ Replace hand towel
- ○ Clean shower drain
- ○ Clean shower door seals
- ○ Clean ceiling cornices
- ○ Dust top of door frames
- ○ Clean blinds/shutters
- ○ Quick clean internal windows
- ○ Clean windowsills
- ○ Deep clean sink
- ○ Deep clean bin

Seasonally
- ○ Clean light fittings
- ○ Clean exhaust fan
- ○ Clean walls
- ○ Dust wall hangings
- ○ Clean window tracks
- ○ Dust plants
- ○ Clean showerheads
- ○ Deep clean cabinets
- ○ Clean skirting boards

Annually
- ○ Deep clean exhaust fan
- ○ Deep clean curtains
- ○ Deep clean internal windows
- ○ Clean external windows

Bathroom Deep Cleaning Checklist

Head start

○ Spray your shower with shower cleaner

Pick up

○ Tidy, pick up and put away clutter

Wash

○ Bath towels
○ Hand towels
○ Bath mats
○ Face washers

Clean

○ Hard water build-up around the taps
○ Light fittings
○ Exhaust fan
○ Ceiling cornices
○ Top of door frames
○ Walls
○ Wall hangings
○ Blinds/shutters
○ Curtains
○ Windows
○ Windowsills and tracks
○ Plants
○ All surfaces
○ Shower
○ Bathtub
○ Bath toys

○ Mirror
○ Makeup brushes
○ Toothbrush holder
○ Soap dispenser
○ Items sitting on top of vanity
○ Bathroom benchtop
○ Bathroom sink
○ Vanity cabinets
○ Light switches
○ Door handles
○ Toilet
○ Bin
○ Skirting boards
○ Floor
○ External windows

Finishing touches

○ Restock supplies
○ Add fresh clean linens
○ Spray with room spray

Laundry Cleaning Checklist

The laundry is typically the room where you wash and dry clothes, store linens and your household cleaners. Keeping this area clean and tidy will help to keep all your appliances and tools running effectively and efficiently.

Daily

- ○ Sort dirty clothes
- ○ Wash and dry a load of washing
- ○ Fold and put away washing
- ○ Quick clean washing machine
- ○ Quick tidy up
- ○ Quick clean sink

Weekly

- ○ Tidy, pick up and put away clutter
- ○ Dust light fittings
- ○ Clean light switches
- ○ Clean door handles
- ○ Dust and clean all surfaces
- ○ Clean benchtop
- ○ Clean splashback
- ○ Deep clean sink
- ○ Clean front loader washing machine door seals
- ○ Clean floor
- ○ Do ironing

Monthly

- ○ Clean ceiling cornices
- ○ Dust top of door frames
- ○ Clean blinds/shutters
- ○ Quick clean internal windows
- ○ Clean windowsills
- ○ Clean washing machine
- ○ Clean dryer
- ○ Clean laundry hampers
- ○ Clean clothesline
- ○ Quick clean cabinets
- ○ Clean vacuum cleaner
- ○ Deep clean sink drains

Seasonally

- ○ Clean light fittings
- ○ Clean walls
- ○ Dust wall hangings
- ○ Clean window tracks
- ○ Dust plants
- ○ Clean behind washing machine
- ○ Clean behind dryer
- ○ Clean iron
- ○ Deep clean cabinets
- ○ Clean skirting boards

Annually

- ○ Deep clean curtains
- ○ Deep clean internal windows
- ○ Clean external windows

Laundry Deep Cleaning Checklist

Head start

○ Run washing machine through a hot vinegar cycle

Pick up

○ Tidy, pick up and put away clutter

Clean

○ Light fittings
○ Ceiling cornices
○ Top of door frames
○ Walls
○ Wall hangings
○ Blinds/shutters
○ Curtains
○ Windows
○ Windowsills and tracks
○ Plants
○ Light switches
○ Door handles
○ All surfaces
○ Behind washing machine
○ Behind dryer
○ Laundry hampers
○ Iron
○ Vacuum cleaner
○ Washing machine
○ Dryer

○ Laundry sink
○ Skirting boards
○ Clothesline
○ Cabinets
○ Floor

Wash

○ Laundry linens
○ Dirty clothes

Finishing touches

○ Restock supplies
○ Add fresh clean linens
○ Spray with room spray

Bedroom Cleaning Checklist

Your bedroom should be a place you feel comfortable in, making it easier for you to relax and rest every night. Make it a priority to create a calm and tidy space, so you can wake up with a clear and relaxed mindset every day.

Daily

- Make bed
- Tidy, pick up and put away all clutter
- Tidy, pick up and put away all clothes
- Put away clean washing
- Quick tidy up

Weekly

- Wash bed sheets and pillow protectors
- Dust light fittings
- Quick clean curtains
- Spot clean internal windows
- Clean light switches
- Clean door handles
- Clean mirrors
- Dust and clean all surfaces
- Dust ornaments
- Quick clean rubbish bin
- Put clean sheets on bed
- Clean floor

Monthly

- Clean quilt cover
- Clean mattress protector
- Clean throw blankets
- Put quilt insert in direct sunlight
- Clean ceiling cornices
- Dust top of door frames
- Clean blinds/shutters
- Quick clean internal windows
- Clean windowsills
- Dust bedhead
- Clean mattress
- Deep clean bin

Seasonally

- Wash quilt insert
- Clean blanket
- Clean pillows
- Clean cushions
- Clean light fittings
- Clean ceiling fan
- Clean air-conditioning filter
- Clean walls
- Dust wall hangings
- Clean window tracks
- Dust plants
- Clean skirting boards
- Freshen up carpets

Annually

- Deep clean carpets
- Deep clean curtains
- Deep clean internal windows
- Deep clean rugs
- Clean external windows

Bedroom Deep Cleaning Checklist

Pick up

- ◯ Tidy, pick up and put away all clutter
- ◯ Tidy, pick up and put away all clothes

Wash

- ◯ Bed sheets
- ◯ Quilt cover and insert
- ◯ Bed blankets
- ◯ Mattress protector
- ◯ Pillows
- ◯ Pillow protector
- ◯ Throw blankets
- ◯ Cushions

Clean

- ◯ Light fittings
- ◯ Ceiling cornices
- ◯ Ceiling fan
- ◯ Air-conditioning filter
- ◯ Top of door frames
- ◯ Walls
- ◯ Wall hangings
- ◯ Blinds/shutters
- ◯ Curtains
- ◯ Windows
- ◯ Windowsills
- ◯ Plants
- ◯ Mirrors
- ◯ Light switches
- ◯ Door handles
- ◯ Bedhead
- ◯ Mattress
- ◯ Ornaments
- ◯ All surfaces
- ◯ Bin
- ◯ Skirting boards
- ◯ Floor rugs
- ◯ Carpet
- ◯ Floor
- ◯ External windows

Finishing touches

- ◯ Place clean bed linen back onto bed
- ◯ Put cushion covers back onto cushions
- ◯ Spray with room spray

Part 3

YOUR CLEANING KIT

With such an abundance of cleaning products
available, what do you actually need?
I've listed all the products and tools to make
cleaning easier and more effective.

Your cleaning kit

Having the right tools makes cleaning so much easier. In this section, I list the essential cleaning supplies you need to tackle different cleaning scenarios around the home. You will find the majority of these items in my shop, Organised HQ.

Making your own cleaning supplies has many benefits. Homemade versions usually cost less than buying ready-made products from the supermarket. You can make them with natural and chemical-free ingredients, plus you reduce landfill. That said, many bought cleaners are becoming more eco-friendly in their packaging and ingredients. Buying ready-made cleaners is often more convenient and they can also be more efficient for some tasks.

When my kids were younger, I made my own cleaners to help reduce the number of toxins in our home, with the added bonus that this approach was budget-friendly. Nowadays there are some great non-toxic cleaning solutions available. I've gathered together a good range at Organised HQ, and I tend to use these products instead of making my own.

Throughout this book I have referenced both homemade cleaners and ready-made so you can decide which you prefer to use.

Ingredients such as ammonia, chlorine, formaldehyde, phthalates, sodium hydroxide and triclosan can cause irritation and allergies in humans and animals. I recommend checking the ingredients label of your cleaning products and always using products as directed.

Bicarbonate of soda

Bicarb soda (also known as baking soda) is a powerful natural product that absorbs and lifts odours. It also provides a gentle abrasive to clean without leaving scratches behind. It partners well with white vinegar. When vacuuming bicarb, it's important to clean your vacuum immediately to remove any build-up.

I keep my bicarb in a shaker, making it easy to sprinkle out the required amount to freshen up a carpet or mattress. Use with a spritz of white vinegar in the kitchen sink, shower, toilet … anywhere there is a stain or odour.

White vinegar

Vinegar is an extremely versatile product. Don't be put off by the odour – I promise you it will disappear in a few minutes. It is effective at dissolving grease and removing dirt, plus it has some disinfectant properties. Great to have when you don't want to use a chemical cleaner.

I use homebrand regular white vinegar found in the salad dressing aisle at the grocery store. Bicarb soda and white vinegar are septic safe.

Lemon juice

In addition to its sweet-smelling fresh scent, lemon juice is one of the best natural cleaners due to its antibacterial properties.

Spray bottle

Reusable spray bottle for DIY cleaning solutions.

Dishwashing liquid

Not just to be used for dishes, it is great for breaking down dirt and cutting through grease and grime build-up throughout the rest of your home. I prefer to use a detergent that isn't coloured to prevent staining carpet or upholstery. Don't be afraid to open the bottle at the grocery store to check.

Floor cleaner

To remove dirt, dust and allergens. Choose a cleaner that is designed for your floor type, some products may vary based on your floor surface.

Multi-purpose cleaner

Use on a range of different surfaces to effectively clean away grease, dirt and stains.

Antibacterial cleaner

To disinfect surfaces around the home, especially in the kitchen and bathroom.

Degreaser cleaner

A stronger formula than multi-purpose cleaner to effectively remove grease splatters in the kitchen.

Stainless-steel cleaner

Removes dirt, bacteria and fingerprints from stainless-steel and chrome-plated surfaces, leaving it streak-free.

Glass cleaner

Removes fingerprints, marks and dust from windows and mirrors.

Bathroom cleaner

Effectively removes soap scum, mould and limescale.

Mould remover

Some bathroom cleaners are not specially formulated to remove mould.
Look for a specific cleaner that cleans away mould.

Toilet cleaner

Keeps the toilet bowl fresh, kills bacteria and removes stains and limescale.

Oven cleaner

Removes stubborn baked-on grease that sometimes can't be removed by
bicarb soda and white vinegar.

Fabric upholstery cleaner

To dissolve and extract spots and stains from upholstery such as lounge
or mattresses.

Cleaning paste

A mild abrasive that is gentle on surfaces but helps to break through the
build-up of stubborn hard-water stains around the sink and tub. It also
removes marks on the walls.

Mild laundry detergent

A mild gentle laundry detergent contains only surface-active agents that
clean dirt and grease from clothes and linens. It should not contain enzymes
or abrasives which are usually found in stronger detergents.

Oxi powder stain remover

A laundry stain-remover powder is a great wash booster, and also helps to
remove grease and grime.

Essential oils

Some essential oils make powerful non-toxic cleaning agents to help clean
surfaces throughout the home, and add fragrance to homemade cleaning
supplies. The most useful are lemon, lavender, eucalyptus and tea tree.

Cleaning cloths

Microfibre cloths are super absorbent and machine-washable so you can use them hundreds of times. Use different-coloured cloths for particular areas of your home to avoid any cross-contamination.

Cleaning sponge

A non-scratch sponge to remove food residue and lift grease off dirty kitchen dishes. The textured surface makes removing build-up on benchtops, cooktops and shower screens easier.

Melamine foam (Magic Eraser)

This dense melamine sponge is lightly abrasive and can remove tough stains with just a little bit of water. Use on walls, doors or even sneakers to remove dirt marks.

Surface cleaning wipes

Use my homemade reusable wipes to wipe away dust, clean light switches and door handles or in the kitchen to clean up spills. Go to page 58 for the recipe.

Dish brush

A brush with a long handle and bristles to help clean dishes and reach the bottom of mugs and cups.

Scrubbing brush

A scrubbing brush will help to loosen up dirt and grime on flyscreens and bins or in the shower.

Duster

A microfibre duster is ideal as it picks up dirt and dust rather than spreading it around. Choose one that has a removable head so you can put it into the washing machine to clean and reuse again.

Blind duster

This is a very handy little cleaning tool that cleans both the top and bottom of each blind slat in one go.

Pillowcase

A dedicated old pillowcase for cleaning fans and cornices around the home.

Window-track cleaning brush

Helps to loosen any dust and dirt sitting inside the tracks, making it easier to vacuum.

Mini cleaning brush

A little tough bristle cleaning brush to get into small areas such as around tapware, shower door tracks, stovetops, etc.

Grout cleaning brush

The tough bristles allow you to scrub the grout between tiles.

Toilet brush

To reach all areas of the toilet, including under the rim. Pick a toilet brush that is durable and easy to keep hygienically clean.

Squeegee

Helps to keep the shower free of mould and mildew. Can also be used to clean windows.

Vacuum cleaner

To collect dirt, dust and allergens from carpeted floors. A vacuum cleaner with attachments is ideal for upholstery, mattresses, skirting boards and other surfaces.

Broom

To pick up crumbs, dirt and dust from non-carpeted floors. Alternatively, you could use a stick vacuum.

Dustpan and brush

Great for quick clean-ups and to pick up dust and dirt after sweeping the floor. The brush from the pan is useful for cleaning dust and dirt off fly-screens.

Mop and bucket

For the final clean of the floor. Choose a mop with an adjustable handle and a removable mop head that is machine washable. It's a bonus if the bucket has or can be placed on wheels so you can easily move it around.

Cobweb broom

Extendable cobweb brooms make it easy to remove cobwebs inside and out. The dome-shaped head makes it easy to get into ceiling cornices, picking up dust and lingering insects.

Silicone gloves

Silicone gloves have a built-in cleaning scrubber to make it easy to pick up pet hair from bed linens or the lounge.

Wool dryer balls

Use wool dryer balls in the clothes dryer to help reduce drying time by creating air pockets for better circulation, allowing hot air to get to the wet clothes easier and more efficiently. They also naturally soften your clothes. Add a few drops of your favourite essential oil to each wool ball to give your laundry a boost of fragrance.

BUILDING A CLEANING CADDY

Build yourself a basic cleaning caddy filled with all the cleaners and tools you use frequently to clean your home. Storing everything in a caddy makes it easy to carry your kit from room to room, and saves you from running back to the laundry for different products. I have two cleaning caddies: one for the bathroom and one for the rest of the house. If you don't have small children, you can leave your bathroom caddy in your bathroom for convenience. Arrange items in your caddy so it's well balanced and avoid cleaners that only do one job (for example, toilet cleaner can be stored next to the toilet).

General cleaning caddy

- ○ Kat's Cleaning Spray (see page 57), antibacterial cleaner or multi-purpose spray
- ○ Bicarb shaker
- ○ Cleaning paste
- ○ Cleaning cloths
- ○ Melamine foam (Magic Eraser)
- ○ Duster
- ○ Blind duster
- ○ Mini cleaning brush
- ○ Window-track cleaning brush

Bathroom cleaning caddy

- ○ Kat's Sparkle Spray (see page 58) or glass cleaner
- ○ Kat's Cleaning Spray (see page 57) or bathroom cleaner
- ○ Kat's Mould Be Gone Spray (see page 57) or mould remover
- ○ Cleaning paste
- ○ Cleaning cloths
- ○ Scrubbing sponges
- ○ Scrubbing brush
- ○ Mini cleaning brush
- ○ Grout cleaning brush
- ○ Squeegee

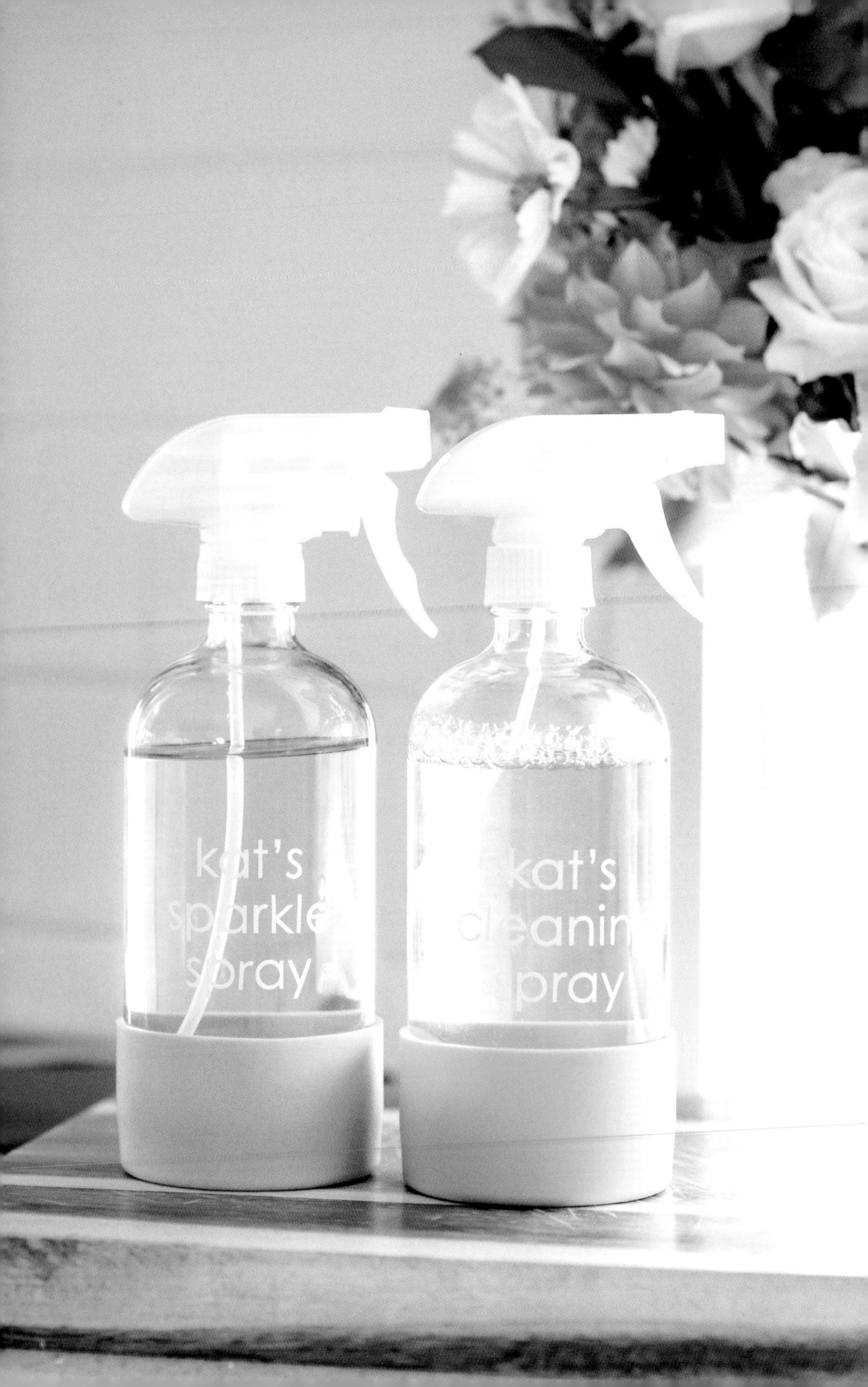
kat's
sparkle
spray
kat's

KAT'S DIY CLEANERS

These cleaning recipes are super easy to make, using basic household products to clean your home. Some cleaners may have the same ingredients, however, pay attention to the differing measurements as this is what makes them effective throughout various surfaces in the home.

Kat's Cleaning Spray

In a spray bottle, combine:

1 cup water
½ cup white vinegar
¼ cup dishwashing liquid

 **Add 8 drops of your favourite essential oil for fragrance to the cleaning spray.**

Kat's Mould Be Gone Spray

In a spray bottle, combine:

1 cup water
1 cup white vinegar
1 teaspoon dishwashing liquid

Kat's Reusable Wipes

Place 12 cleaning cloths in an airtight container.
In a jug, combine:

1 cup water

1 cup white vinegar

2 teaspoons dishwashing liquid

12 drops of lavender essential oil

5 drops of your favourite essential oil

Pour the mixture over the cloths and seal the container.
Use within a week.

Kat's tip Using vinegar and lavender essential oil gives the wipes antibacterial properties to help clean away germs.

Kat's Sparkle Spray

In a spray bottle, combine:

1 cup white vinegar

1 cup water

The acidic composition of vinegar acts quickly to break down the film that frequently accumulates on glass surfaces too. Add 8 drops of lemon essential oil to the sparkle spray to help deter creepy crawly insects.

Lemon Soda Paste

In a bowl, combine:

½ cup bicarb soda

2 tablespoons lemon juice (or more if needed to achieve the right consistency)

For an extra boost, spray area with vinegar shortly before wiping away the lemon soda paste. When cleaning the oven, add a few drops of dishwashing liquid to the paste.

Fresh Carpet Sprinkle

In a shaker, combine:

½ cup bicarb soda

20 drops of lemon essential oil

Kat's Washing Machine Spray

In a spray bottle, combine:

2 cups white vinegar

30 drops of lemon eucalyptus essential oil

Floor Cleaner (without vinegar)

Half-fill a mop bucket with room-temperature water, and add:

1–2 teaspoons dishwashing liquid, then gently stir.

Use this floor cleaner solution for laminate, hardwood, bamboo, stone, concrete and linoleum floors. (Vinegar can dull or stain polished or sealed hardwood floors.)

Floor Cleaner (with vinegar)

Half-fill a mop bucket with room-temperature water, and add:

1 teaspoon dishwashing liquid

½ cup white vinegar, then gently stir.

Floor cleaner with vinegar is best used on vinyl, tile and cork flooring.

Laundry Stripping Mix

Half-fill the bathtub with hot water, and add:

½ cup laundry detergent powder

¼ cup borax

¼ cup washing soda

Kat's Mattress Spray

In a spray bottle, combine.

1 cup water

1 cup white vinegar

8 drops of lemon eucalyptus essential oil

8 drops of lavender essential oil

8 drops of peppermint essential oil

Spider Repellent Spray

In a spray bottle, combine:

1 cup water

15 drops of peppermint essential oil

15 drops of lemon essential oil

Part 4

HOW
TO
CLEAN

I've broken down all the general home
cleaning tasks into easy manageable steps to
help you quickly and efficiently get the job
done so you can spend more time relaxing or
doing the things you love most.

AIR-CONDITIONING FILTERS

Air-conditioning filters catch dust and other airborne pollutants and bacteria. Regular cleaning of the air filters will improve the machine's efficiency, lower its electricity usage and prevent mould. It will also improve the quality of the air you breathe when the system is running.

Always read the manufacturer's instructions for more detailed directions before you clean. You might also consider getting your air-conditioner system professionally serviced and cleaned annually.

KIT

Dustpan brush or vacuum cleaner with small brush attachment

Dishwashing liquid

Cleaning cloth

STEPS

- Lift up the main large cover and remove the filters.
- Take the filters outside or place in the laundry sink, and use a dustpan brush to gently brush away dust. Alternatively, use the vacuum to remove dust from the filter.
- If the filters are grimy, wash with warm water and dishwashing liquid.
- Rinse the filter well with clean water. Allow filter to air-dry completely.
- Clean away dust from filter housing using the dustpan brush.
- Put the filters back once thoroughly dry.
- Vacuum floor to pick up any dust that has fallen.

HOW OFTEN?

Seasonally, or monthly if you use your air-conditioning regularly.

BATH TOWELS

There is nothing like wrapping yourself in a fresh clean towel after you have had a bath or shower. It's easy to assume that because you're drying your clean body with the towel that your towel will stay reasonably clean. Wrong! Towels need to be washed weekly as they absorb a lot of water, remain damp for hours, and dirty hands get wiped on them, which all leads to a breeding ground for bacteria, germs and mould. This is why it's important to always hang bath towels evenly over a towel rail to dry after each use. Follow these same steps to wash hand towels bath mats and face washers.

If you find your towels have an odour after they are dried, it may be because they were left too long in the washing machine or an indication that your washing machine needs a clean (see pages 193–5).

In my bathroom I have the same coloured bath towels and coordinating bath mat, but I soon learnt that having three towels all the same colour in the kids' bathroom was too confusing. After they dried themselves, they dropped the towels on the floor and ran off, and I had no idea whose towel belonged to whom. To fix this, each of the kids has their own coloured bath towel.

KIT

Laundry detergent

White vinegar

Essential oil

Oxi powder stain remover

Wool dryer balls

STEPS

- Wash white, coloured and dark towels separately in the washing machine to maintain their colour. Do not wash with clothes. Don't overload the washing machine – it's best to give your towels plenty of room.

- Use warm water with laundry detergent.

- Use ½ cup vinegar and a few drops of your favourite essential oil instead of fabric softener. Fabric softener leaves a build-up on the towel fibres and reduces absorbency.

- Add oxi powder stain remover to boost colour and help remove grease and grime.

- Wash on a gentle wash cycle which lowers the spin speed.

- Optional: run an extra rinse cycle. This helps to remove any build-up of detergent (which makes towels scratchy and less absorbent).

- Remove from the washing machine, shake, then stretch all edges of the towel to help re-shape them. Do not leave your towels too long in the washing machine.

- For the fluffiest towels, dry in your clothes dryer using wool dryer balls with a few drops of essential oil to add fragrance and help the air circulate. Alternatively, dry on the clothesline.

HOW OFTEN?

Daily – for regularly used hand towels.

Weekly – or more often if humidity is high in your home (and towels don't dry between use), family members are unwell, have skin allergies or acne.

 **Colour-code bath towels for the kids to prevent arguments and extra washing.**

THE BATHROOM SINK

Makeup, blobs of toothpaste and soap spills can quickly build up in the sink, with limescale and soap scum pooling around the drain and tapware. A daily spot clean can prevent an unsightly build-up, and a weekly quick clean will remove bacteria, grime and unpleasant smells.

KIT

Kat's Cleaning Spray (see page 57) or bathroom cleaner

Cleaning cloths

Mini cleaning brush

Cleaning paste or Lemon Soda Paste (see page 59)

White vinegar

Bicarb soda

STEPS

Quick clean

- Spray tapware, sink, drain and benchtop with cleaner and wipe with a cleaning cloth. Use a mini cleaning brush to get into those hard-to-reach areas.

- To remove stubborn build-up around tapware and the sink drain, dab on some cleaning paste and leave for 10 minutes. If using Lemon Soda Paste, spray with vinegar and leave for a further 5 minutes. Use a mini brush to remove build-up.

- Rinse with a damp cloth.

- Polish tapware with a dry cleaning cloth.

Deep clean

- If possible, remove the drain cover. Some drain covers cannot be removed.

- Soak the sink plug and drain cover in 1 cup vinegar for 5 minutes.

- Scrub with a mini brush to remove any build-up.

- Spray drain with cleaner. Dab some cleaning paste on a mini brush and scrub inside to remove mould build-up.

- Rinse drain. Clean around the top of the plug hole with cleaning spray and a cloth.

- Place the drain cover back.

- Sprinkle ¼ cup bicarb soda down the drain followed by ½ cup vinegar to freshen. Sit for 15 minutes. Wash away with water.

To prevent mineral deposits, keep water from pooling around the taps by regularly wiping them down with a cloth or towel.

HOW OFTEN?
Daily – spot clean.
Weekly – quick clean.
Monthly – deep clean.

THE BATHTUB

The bathtub needs a regular clean to remove soap scum, limescale, mineral deposit, body oil, dust and dirt – especially if you have kids. I prefer to naturally clean the bathtub, so those who bathe in it are safe and free from chemicals and toxins.

KIT

Kat's Mould Be Gone Spray (see page 57) or mould remover

Grout cleaning brush

Cleaning cloths

Cleaning paste or Lemon Soda Paste (see page 59)

Dishwashing liquid

Bicarb soda

White vinegar

Kat's Cleaning Spray (see page 57) or bathroom cleaning spray

Mini cleaning brush

STEPS

- Remove all toys and toiletries from the tub.

- Deal with any mould. Spray Mould Be Gone Spray or mould remover on visible mould patches. After 5 minutes, use the grout cleaning brush to remove. Rinse area.

- Wet the entire surface of the bathtub.

- Use a cleaning cloth to apply cleaning paste to the dirt ring around the bathtub and stubborn build-up around tapware. Alternatively, add a few drops of dishwashing liquid to Lemon Soda Paste (this will help it cling to the side of the bath tub), then smear paste on the side of the tub and around tapware.

- Sprinkle bicarb over the bottom of the tub, spray the entire tub with vinegar and watch it fizz. Sit for 10 minutes. Alternatively, use a cleaning spray.

- Use a cloth to scrub away the dirt from the top, side and bottom of tub as well as tapware. Spritz with more cleaning spray if needed, working in a circular motion to remove stubborn stains. Use a mini brush to get into hard-to-reach spots.

- Rinse the tub and wipe with a clean cloth.

Spa bath

- Dab cleaning paste or Lemon Soda Paste around each jet.

- Sprinkle bicarb over the bottom of the tub, spray the entire tub with vinegar and watch it fizz. Sit for 10 minutes.

- Fill the spa bath with warm water, to cover the jets. Pour 2–3 cups vinegar into the water.

- Run the jets for 3–5 minutes.

- Empty, then spray the tub with cleaning spray and wipe over with a cleaning cloth.

HOW OFTEN?

Weekly – bathtub (and wipe over spa bath).

Seasonally – spa bath.

BED LINENS

Dust, dirt, skin cells, body oil, fluid, sweat, odour – starting to feel a little icky at the thought that this is what you are sleeping on each night?! All this may be lingering on your bed linens, such as bed sheets, pillow and mattress protectors. Dust mites like to feed off dead skin flakes found there, and this can aggravate allergies.

Pillowcases can also be a breeding ground for bacteria. If you or your children suffer from oily or acne-prone skin, you may want to consider changing the pillowcases more often. It's best to wash your bed sheets and pillowcases separately from your other clothes and linen.

 *Kat's tip*

My children suffer from allergies, so I wash bed sheets weekly in hot water, which helps kill dust mites.

KIT

Laundry detergent

White vinegar

Essential oil

Oxi powder stain remover

Wool dryer balls

STEPS

- Wash bed sheets, pillow and mattress protectors in the washing machine using cold water with laundry detergent. After illness and to help ease allergies, wash in hot water.

- Don't overload the washing machine – it's best to give your linens plenty of room. If you have a top loading washing machine, to prevent damaging your sheets, do not wrap the sheets around the agitator.

- Add oxi powder stain remover to boost colour and help remove grease and grime.

- Use ½ cup vinegar and a few drops of your favourite essential oil instead of fabric softener.

- Dry on the clothesline. Alternatively, dry in your clothes dryer using wool dryer balls with a few drops of essential oil to add fragrance and help the air circulate.

HOW OFTEN?

Weekly – bed sheets and pillow protectors, more often for humid weather or night sweaters.

Monthly – mattress protector.

Nobody likes folding sheets – I am pretty sure that's a fact. I strip the beds first thing in the morning and get the linens through the wash and dried in the same day. Then I simply make the bed that evening with the fresh sheets I just cleaned. No folding required!

Dust mites

Dust mites like to hide in household furnishings such as sheets, doonas, quilts, pillows, cushions, mattresses, woollen underlays, curtains, teddies, carpets and rugs.

Dust mites are microscopic, virtually invisible insects, that live on animal and human skin cells and thrive in warm temperatures and high humidity. Their droppings contain a protein-like substance that is known to trigger asthma, eczema and other allergies. Scary fact: there can be up to 10,000 of these little insects per square metre in an average home – I shudder at the thought!

BLANKETS

A blanket on the bed is ideal for keeping you cosy and warm during the cooler months. Always check instructions before washing them.

Woollen and cashmere blankets especially will need extra care. Do not wash on a temperature higher than 30°C and always choose a gentle cycle with a mild wool washing detergent. Do not spin. Dry flat, in the shade.

KIT

Mild laundry detergent

White vinegar

Wool dryer balls

STEPS

- Wash the blanket by itself in the washing machine on a regular cold cycle with mild laundry detergent. Don't use too much detergent, as too much will stick to and damage the blanket's fibres.

- Use ½ cup vinegar and a few drops of your favourite essential oil instead of fabric softener.

- Dry on the clothesline in the sun, as the sunlight acts as a natural way to remove odours and kill bacteria. Drying your blanket may take some time, Alternatively, if care instructions advise your blanket can be tumble dried and it fits in the dryer, dry at a low temperature with wool dryer balls to help the air circulate.

HOW OFTEN?

Seasonally – or more regularly if you do not use a top sheet when sleeping.

BLINDS AND SHUTTERS

Dust and dirt from outside can settle on the blinds and shutters through open windows. If windows are left open during the wet season, mould spores may appear on your blinds. It's important to not use excessive amounts of water when cleaning as this will cause swelling and stain wooden blinds/shutters.

KIT

Duster or blind duster

Cleaning cloth or paper towel

Kat's Mould Be Gone Spray (see page 57), multi-purpose cleaner or Kat's Reusable Wipes (see page 58)

Mini cleaning brush

STEPS

- Remember the Cleaning Cha Cha (see page 15). Start at the top and work your way across each slat until you get to the bottom.

- Use a duster or blind duster to remove dust on the top and bottom of each slat.

- To remove dirt spots or mould spores, lightly spray a dry cleaning cloth or paper towel with cleaner or use wipes to carefully remove the dirt build-up.

- Use a mini brush to get into cracks, crevices and hinges.

- Clean the windowsill to remove any dropped dust and dirt.

HOW OFTEN?
Monthly.

CARPETS

Residue, dirt and dust from windows and doors left open, our feet and our pets' paws can quickly build up in the carpet and leave it smelly and drab. Regularly cleaning your carpet will keep it fresh and help extend its life. If you have young children or pets, it is worth purchasing a small handheld upholstery cleaner to combat stains.

KIT

Vacuum cleaner

Paper towel or cleaning cloth

Kat's Cleaning Spray (see page 57)

Bicarb soda

White vinegar

Fresh Carpet Sprinkle (see page 59)

STEPS

Quick clean

- Use your vacuum's strongest suction to clean your floors. Vacuum slowly, overlapping strokes in a forwards and backwards motion.

Spot clean – dried-on mess (pet, mud, vomit)

- Use a paper towel to pick up as much solid matter from the mess as you can.

- Vacuum up remaining dried-on mess.

- If necessary, remove the attachment from your vacuum and use the nozzle to go over the area, left to right, backwards and forwards, several times to pick up all the dried particles stuck between the carpet pile.

- Then proceed with the spot clean steps on page 80 to remove the stain.

Shoes or no shoes?

This has been a controversial topic on The Organised Housewife over the years! It's each to their own in your own home with pros and cons for both sides. Personally, I prefer visitors to leave their shoes at the door when coming into our home. I don't like dirt being walked into the house and onto the carpets (ours are light in colour and show dirt really easily). The kids wear shoes (thongs) outside to protect their feet from bindis in the grass and then leave them at the door to ensure they don't bring dirt onto the carpets. As I get older, I'm finding that I can't walk around the house barefoot, so I have a dedicated pair of shoes that are for indoors only.

Spot clean – liquid (drinks, urine, pet)

- Use a paper towel or cleaning cloth to dab the area to pick up as much liquid as possible. DO NOT RUB the area: dab/blot only. Rubbing will damage the carpet pile and can spread the stain further.

- If the area is stained, lightly spray with the cleaning spray, sit for 5 minutes, then dab/blot the area. Repeat as necessary to pick up the stain.

- To help remove the odour, sprinkle the area with bicarb soda, then lightly spray with vinegar. Leave to sit for 30 minutes or until the area has dried. Vacuum up the powder from the carpet. Clean vacuum to remove any bicarb build-up.

Freshen up

- Lightly shake the Carpet Sprinkle over high-traffic areas and let sit for 30 minutes.

- Vacuum the area to pick up the bicarb soda. Clean the vacuum to remove any bicarb build-up.

Deep clean

- Shampooing is advised if you have pets or smoke in the home. This can also help extend the life of your carpet. Hire a carpet cleaner from a large hardware store or local supermarket, or consider getting professionals in.

Only use bicarb soda on dry carpets, not wet. Keep pets and small children away from the carpets when treating, as the bicarb soda may irritate their paws, feet or eyes.

HOW OFTEN?

Immediately – spot clean spills.
Weekly – quick clean.
Seasonally – freshen up.
Annually – deep clean.

Doormats help keep dirt out

Doormats aren't just a home accessory. They are an essential part of keeping the floor clean by stopping the dirt coming inside. Place a doormat at all the external doors – front, back, garage and laundry – to prevent dirt embedding into your carpet and making the cleaning process longer and harder. If you have pets, it's a good idea to keep an old towel by the door for wiping dirty paws.

CEILING CORNICES

Over time you may find that cobwebs appear on your ceiling cornices, which then collect dirt and dust. This area can be a little tricky to clean as it's up high and often gets neglected as one of those 'one day' tasks … until the day you look up and the cobwebs are starting to dangle and you know you have to get rid of them.

Before you start, inspect your ceilings to see if there are any live spiders. If they are the nasty kind, like a redback, you may need to call in the pest control professionals.

I recommend using a facemask over your nose and mouth along with eye protection (you could use sunglasses) to protect yourself from falling dust and dirt.

KIT

Cobweb broom

Pillowcase

Cleaning cloth

Lemon essential oil

Vacuum cleaner with brush attachment

STEPS

- Glide a cobweb broom around the cornices to remove all dust and cobwebs.

- To deter creepy crawlies from coming back, wrap a pillowcase or cloth around the head of the cobweb broom and add a couple of drops of lemon essential oil. Glide the broom over the cleaned cornice.

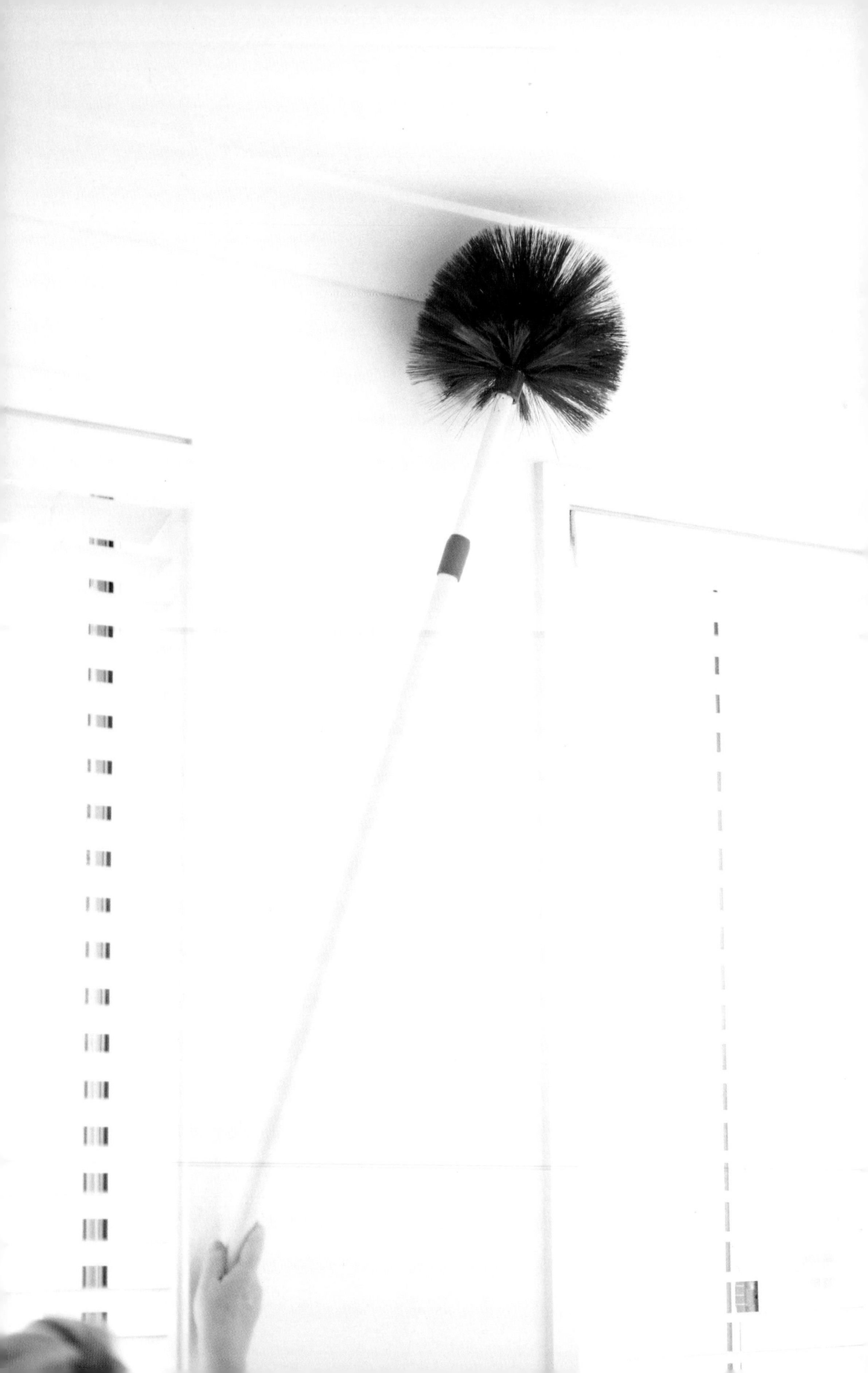

- Sometimes bugs can leave a mess on the ceiling cornices. Spot clean only using a light mist of water on a cleaning cloth, gently dabbing the area.

- Dust and vacuum the room to pick up any dropped dust or cobwebs.

- Shake the pillowcase outside or over the laundry sink to remove all the dust. Clean in the washing machine using hot water and laundry detergent.

To clean the cobweb broom

- Remove the head, if possible. Put on a glove, take broom outside or place over the laundry sink, shake it vigorously and run glove over bristles to remove dust and dirt.

- For a deep clean, fill a sink with warm water and dishwashing liquid, submerge the head of the brush and swish to clean. Use a glove to run your hand over bristles, helping to remove cobwebs. Empty the sink and rinse the broom with clean water. Shake off excess water and allow to air-dry.

HOW OFTEN?
Monthly.

CEILING FANS

Fans tend to gather a build-up of dust that settles when they're not in use, especially over winter. Turning the fan on and spreading this dust can then trigger allergies. Regular cleaning will not only ensure a longer life for your fan, but it will also keep the air in your home cleaner.

Dust build-up can also be the reason for squeaky fan noises (which are very annoying throughout the night). I keep an old pillowcase in my cleaning cupboard dedicated to cleaning fans. It's a clever trick to prevent the dust from spreading throughout the room. If you have allergies or are sensitive to dust, cover your face with a mask while cleaning.

KIT

Pillowcase

Cleaning cloth

Kat's Cleaning Spray (see page 57), multi-purpose cleaner or Kat's Reusable Wipes (see page 58)

STEPS

- Ensure your fan is switched off.

- Slide the pillowcase over fan blades so that the blade is inside the pillowcase.

- To help prevent dust from falling out, scrunch the opening of the pillowcase around the blade. Using your hands, press the fabric of the pillowcase against the side of the blades so the dust releases and falls into the pillowcase. Repeat on each fan blade.

- If needed, use a cleaning cloth and a light spritz of cleaner (or wipes) to remove any extra dust build-up.

- Shake the pillowcase outside or over the laundry sink to remove all the dust. Turn the case inside out to make sure all the dust is cleaned away.

- Clean the pillowcase in the washing machine using hot water and laundry detergent.

HOW OFTEN?
Seasonally – or you may need to clean more often if you live in an area with dust stirring regularly outside.

CLEANING CLOTHS

Reusable cleaning cloths are great, but they too need to be cleaned to wash away the dirt, dust and residue from the cleaning solution. Avoid using fragranced detergents and fabric softeners to clean them, as this can coat the fibres of the cloth and make them less effective. When you notice your cloths are no longer picking up dust and dirt effectively, it's time to throw them away and replace them.

KIT

Mild laundry detergent

Oxi powder stain remover

White vinegar

STEPS

- Always shake and rinse each cloth after each use to remove the cleaning solution. Hang to dry over a bucket or on the side of the sink (so you don't confuse it with a clean cloth) to avoid mould. When you have enough dirty cloths, run a load of washing.

- Wash in hot water with a small amount of mild laundry detergent, oxi powder (optional) and ½ cup vinegar in the fabric softener dispenser. Do not wash with towels or clothes as the lint from these items can damage the fibres on your cloths.

- Hang to dry in direct sunlight if you can, as the sunlight acts as a natural way of killing bacteria.

- If using your clothes dryer, ensure you clean out the fluff filters first to avoid lint settling on your cleaning cloths.

HOW OFTEN?

After each use.

THE CLOTHESLINE

The clothesline is exposed to all external elements and picks up environmental dust and dirt, spider webs and more. It's important to clean it regularly as you don't want to put your freshly washed clothes and linens on a dirty line. This is also a good time to inspect your pegs to prevent them from marking your clothes. To stop pegs from deteriorating, keep them out of the weather when not in use.

KIT

Cleaning cloths

Cobweb broom

Kat's Cleaning Spray (see page 57), multi-purpose cleaner or Kat's Reusable Wipes (see page 58)

Spider Repellent Spray (see page 61)

STEPS

- Use a dry cloth or cobweb broom and wipe away any spider webs.
- Generously spray cleaning spray onto a cloth, and wipe over each line removing all dirt build-up. Allow to dry.
- Inspect your pegs.
- If you have spiders sitting on your clothesline, spray some of my natural spider repellent onto a cloth and wipe over each of the lines to help prevent them from coming back.

HOW OFTEN?
Monthly.

CURTAINS

Curtains get dirty very easily. While they may look clean, curtains collect dirt and dust coming through the windows, hands transfer dirt and oils onto them as curtains are regularly opened and closed, and they absorb smells from around the home, from pets and cooking. All of which leaves them less than clean and fresh. If you suffer from environmental allergies, washing your curtains regularly may help to ease your symptoms.

If your curtains are large and heavy (as a lot of blockout curtains can be), you may find it easier to deep clean during the warmer months so the curtains dry easily or get them dry cleaned. Please check your curtains for washing instructions and follow carefully. Only wash two curtain panels at a time.

KIT

Vacuum cleaner with brush attachment

Mild laundry detergent

Cleaning cloths

White vinegar

Oxi powder stain remover

STEPS

Quick clean

- Heavy fabric curtains: using the vacuum with the brush attachment, vacuum curtains to remove loose dirt, dust and hair.

- Sheer curtains: lightly bunch the curtain and give it a gentle shake to remove dust. Wait 10 minutes for the dust to settle before dusting furniture and vacuuming the floor around the room.

- Spot-clean stains: using water and a mild laundry detergent, blot the spot with a damp cloth and dab with vinegar to help remove the stain.

Deep clean

- Inspect curtains for stains and pre-treat using the spot-clean method above.

- Carefully take off the curtain from the rod, removing any hooks, rings and curtain weights. Shake outside or over the bathtub to remove any dust and hair.

- To handwash, fill a laundry sink or bathtub with cold water, and add laundry detergent plus oxi powder to boost fabric. Swish water to dissolve cleaners. Submerge your curtain, swirl around the water and soak the curtains for 5 minutes. Do not rub or wring the fabric. Empty the tub and rinse curtains thoroughly with clean water. Squeeze as much water out of the curtains as you can. Place a large towel onto a flat surface and lay your curtain on the towel. Roll the towel up with the curtain inside and sit for a few minutes to help absorb most of the water.

- To gentle machine wash, place the curtains in the washing machine. To avoid crushing, do not overload the washer. Wash on a gentle spin cycle using cold water and laundry detergent. Immediately remove from the washing machine to prevent creases.

- Dust and clean the curtain rod, and deep clean the window and sill (see page 201) before rehanging the curtain.

- To dry, hang on the washing line with the back of the curtain to the sun to prevent colour fading. Do not fold them as this will create a crease. If you do not wish to iron, rehang curtains inside when still slightly damp.

- To iron (only for ironable fabric), carefully iron while slightly damp on the wrong side of the fabric to keep creases from setting into the fabric. Stretch seams gently while ironing to avoid puckering.

HOW OFTEN?
Weekly – **quick clean.**
Annually – **deep clean.**

CUSHION COVERS

Decorative cushions can get dirty, even if you don't use them. Dust settles, fingers mark and pets may lay on them when you're not looking. My top tip for a quick and easy clean is to use a silicone glove to pick up pet hair.

KIT

Laundry detergent

White vinegar

Vacuum cleaner with small brush attachment

Bicarb soda

STEPS

Cotton covers

- Remove the inserts.
- Wash the covers in the washing machine on a cold gentle cycle with laundry detergent and ½ cup vinegar in the fabric softener dispenser.
- Line dry inside out.
- Iron on a delicate setting.

Knitted or woollen covers

- Remove the inserts.
- Handwash the covers in cold water with a gentle laundry detergent.
- Dry flat.
- Do not iron.

Fur covers

- Remove the inserts.

- Handwash the cover in cold water with a gentle laundry detergent.
- Line dry in the sunshine.
- Do not iron.

Outdoor covers

- Spot clean with warm soapy water.
- Line dry in the sunshine.
- Do not iron.

Polyester cushion inserts

- Wash in the washing machine on a cold gentle cycle with laundry detergent and ½ cup vinegar in the fabric softener dispenser. Wash with towels to help keep the washing machine balanced.
- Shake the insert to evenly distribute the fluffy insides.
- Line dry in the sunshine.

Feather or down cushion inserts

- Do not wash, as this can damage the feathers.
- If the insert is smelly, sprinkle it with bicarb soda. Sit for 30 minutes, shake the excess off outside or over the laundry sink.
- Dip a cleaning cloth in warm soapy water and wring out, then wipe over the insert.
- Lay flat in the sun to dry.

HOW OFTEN?
Seasonally.

THE DISHES

I tossed up whether to add dishes as a step-by-step task, then I decided to address it because there is one step in particular that I know many people do, even though it's not required. Can you guess what it is? Rinsing the dishes before putting them in the dishwasher. The truth is that most modern dish-washers have a sensor program to detect how dirty your dishes are with no extra rinsing efforts needed.

Once the dishes are clean, my preference is to let them air-dry overnight. I put them away the next day when I make my morning coffee. I'm not keen on using a tea towel if I don't have to, as I prefer to avoid spreading any lurking germs, and it is one less thing I have to do.

KIT

Dishwashing liquid

Dish brush

Cleaning sponge

Dishwasher cleaner and rinse aid

STEPS

Handwashing

- Scrape leftover food off the dishes into a bin or garbage disposal.

- Rinse extra dirty or greasy dishes with hot water.

- Fill the sink with hot water and dishwashing liquid.

- Wash the dishes in order, from cleanest to dirtiest, typically washing glasses (using a dish brush to clean inside), plates and cutlery first as they stack nicely in the dish rack. Finish with pots and pans.

Beer glasses

If beer glasses are not cleaned properly, the next glass
of beer may not have the same clarity, head
retention, carbonation or correct aroma.
Here are my tips:

- Always handwash beer glasses.

- Have a separate 'beer glass only' cleaning sponge or brush
  to prevent grease and grime transferring onto the glass.

- Wash your beer glasses in hot soapy water with
  the designated sponge or brush before doing the
  rest of the dishes.

- Rinse thoroughly under hot water to remove all soap suds.

- Place glasses upside down on a dish rack allowing
  ventilation.

- Air-dry – do not dry with a tea towel.

- Use your cleaning sponge to clean dishes, keeping the dishes underwater as you clean them.

- If your water becomes greasy, empty and refill the sink.

- Place the dishes in the dish rack to air-dry to avoid the need to dry with a tea towel.

- Empty the sink and clean (see page 131) to rinse away any grease or food.

For burnt-on food, dip your baking pan or tray into a sink of water, then remove. Sprinkle with cookware cleanser or bicarb soda and sit for 60 seconds. Use a cleaning sponge to lift any baked-on food particles. Repeat if necessary.

Dishwasher

- Scrape leftover food off the dish into the bin or garbage disposal.

- Place cups, small dishes and large utensils on the top rack.

- Place plates and larger dishes on the bottom rack, pointing all plates and bowls in the same direction to make good use of the space.

- Mix your utensils in the cutlery holder to prevent them from nesting together and not cleaning properly.

- Do not put crystal, fine china, wood, pewter, bronze or brass dishes in the dishwasher – they should be handwashed.

- Add your desired dishwasher cleaner and run cycle.

- Use rinse aid to support the drying process.

- When emptying the dishwasher, always start with emptying the bottom rack to prevent the water pooled on top of the items (coffee cups) from dripping onto the dried items underneath.

HOW OFTEN?
Daily.

Wooden chopping boards

Do not immerse wooden chopping boards in water
as this will cause them to crack or warp, and become
breeding grounds for bacteria. Instead, handwash
with a damp cloth and warm soapy water.

To dry, place in a position that will allow air to
circulate around the board. Lightly spray with white
vinegar and wipe with a damp cloth to disinfect.

THE DISHWASHER

The dishwasher has to be one of the best inventions ever made! It saves you time standing over a kitchen sink, especially after you've been entertaining and have lots of dirty dishes, glasses and utensils. A dishwasher needs to be looked after and maintained well for it to function properly and provide you with the best dish cleaning service.

KIT

Cleaning cloth

Kat's Cleaning Spray (see page 57), multi-purpose cleaner or Kat's Reusable Wipes (see page 58)

Mini brush

Kat's Sparkle Spray (see page 58) or stainless-steel cleaner

Dishwashing liquid

White vinegar

Bicarb soda

Paper towel

Olive oil

STEPS

Quick clean

- Spray door seals, rim buttons and handles with cleaning spray and wipe with a cloth (or use wipes) to remove dirt build-up. Use a mini brush to help remove stubborn grime. Polish with Kat's Sparkle Spray or stainless-steel cleaner to remove fingerprints.

- Clean filter. Fill up the kitchen sink with warm soapy water. Remove the filter and rinse under hot water to remove built-up gunk. Place in the sink.

- Use a mini brush to remove trapped particles from the mesh screen and plastic frame. Rinse and place back in the dishwasher, making sure you have locked it in place.

- Remove any food caught in the cutlery basket/tray.

Deep clean

- Clean the dishwasher following the previous steps.

- Place a jug filled with 1 cup vinegar onto the top rack of the dishwasher – this will help to remove grease and limescale in the machine and pipes. To freshen the smell of your dishwasher, sprinkle 1 cup bicarb soda on the bottom. Turn your dishwasher onto the economy setting, using the hottest temperature, and run through a cycle. Once the cycle has finished, use a cloth to wipe away all internal gunk.

- Wipe down the outside of your dishwasher and any surrounding cupboards or walls that may have splutters from dirty dishes.

- If your dishwasher is stainless steel, polish using a paper towel with a splash of olive oil. Wipe in the direction of the grain, adding more oil to the towel when necessary.

HOW OFTEN?

Daily – remove bits of food.

Weekly – quick clean.

Monthly – deep clean.

DOOR HANDLES

Like light switches, door handles are one of the most frequently touched areas in the home. As such, they can harbour a lot of dirt and germs, ready for the next person that touches them. Keep them clean with the easy method below.

KIT

Kat's Cleaning Spray (see page 57), multi-purpose cleaner or Kat's Reusable Wipes (see page 58)

Cleaning cloths

STEPS

• Spray cleaning spray onto the door handle and surrounding areas, and wipe with a cloth to remove dirt, fingerprints and germs. Alternatively, use wipes.

HOW OFTEN?

Weekly – or daily if there is any illness in the home.

THE DRYER

If you are finding that your clothes are taking longer to dry, your dryer may need a clean. Cleaning the lint catcher after each load will help lower your electricity bill, reduce the risk of fire and keep the dryer running efficiently.

KIT

Vacuum cleaner with small brush attachment

Dishwashing liquid

Mini brush

White vinegar

Cleaning cloths

Kat's Cleaning Spray (see page 57) or multi-purpose cleaner

Cleaning paste or Lemon Soda Paste (see page 59)

Dustpan and brush and broom, for behind the dryer

Mop and bucket, for behind the dryer

STEPS

Lint screen

- Remove the lint screen and remove lint build-up.

- Vacuum the screen and the space where the screen sits, using the small brush attachment.

- Fill the sink up with hot soapy water and use a mini brush to remove any excess lint build-up from the screen.

- Rinse and air-dry thoroughly before returning to the dryer.

Dryer drum

- Spray equal parts vinegar and water into the dryer drum. Wipe with a cloth to remove any build-up from fabric softener. Leave the door open to air-dry.

Exterior

- Spray with cleaning spray and use a cloth to remove any scuff marks.
- Use cleaning paste or Lemon Soda Paste for stubborn marks, and wipe clean with a damp cleaning cloth.

Behind the dryer

- Unplug the dryer and carefully pull it away from the wall.
- Using your dustpan brush or a dry cleaning cloth, wipe away any dust sitting on the electrical cord and on the back of the dryer. If dust is stuck on, carefully use the brush attachment on your vacuum cleaner to remove it.
- Use a broom and dustpan to sweep up the dust and dirt under the dryer. Alternatively, you could use your vacuum, but it could be sticky and you don't really want that in your vacuum. Mop the floor.
- Move the dryer back into place and plug it back in.

HOW OFTEN?

Every use – remove lint from screen.

Monthly – lint screen, dryer drum and exterior.

Seasonally – behind the dryer.

DUSTING

Dusting is important as it helps to reduce the risk of allergies. You may have heard the phrase 'I'm cleaning my house from top to bottom'. This is because if you start dusting at the top of a bookshelf, for example, any dust that spreads or falls will be collected as you work your way down. But if you begin at the bottom and go up, the dust will fall onto the surface you have already cleaned. This is why we do the Cleaning Cha Cha (see page 15) and I always suggest cleaning your floors last in your routine because you will then pick up the last of any lingering dust.

As beautiful as a feather duster is, it does a surprisingly terrible job at dusting, as it moves and spreads the dust rather than picking it up. It is best to use a microfibre duster or damp cloth.

There are two ways to dust:

Dry dusting, where you use the duster or cloth to pick up the dust.

Wet dusting, where you spray the surface with cleaning spray and wipe with a cloth. To help prevent mould, ensure your surface is dry before placing items back.

KIT

Duster

**Kat's Cleaning Spray (see page 57), multi-purpose cleaner or
Kat's Reusable Wipes (see page 58)**

Cleaning cloth

Vacuum cleaner with small brush attachment

Soft bristle paint brush

Dishwashing liquid, for cleaning duster

STEPS

- Remove all items from the surface.
- For dry dusting, dust the surface with a duster. For wet dusting, spray with cleaner and wipe dust away with a cleaning cloth, or use reusable wipes.
- Dust the item before returning it.
- If you are wet dusting with a cleaner and cloth, make sure the surface is dry before placing items back.

Bookshelves

- Using the small brush attachment on your vacuum cleaner, vacuum the top and spine of the books to pick up dust.
- Deep clean seasonally: remove the books and dust the shelf with a duster or damp cleaning cloth. Ensure that the shelf is completely dry before placing books back.

Electrical equipment

- Unplug the equipment first.
- Use a duster to get into the crevices.
- Use a cleaning cloth to dust the cords.

House plants (real and faux)

- For small delicate houseplants, use a soft bristle paint brush.
- For larger leaves, remove dust with a duster or use a slightly damp (water only) cleaning cloth; support under the leaf with one hand, then very gently wipe over the leaf to clean away dust.
- Do not take plants outside and spray them with a hose, as this can create a mess.

To clean the duster

- Take the duster outside and shake it vigorously.
- If your duster has a removable head, remove it from the handle.

- Fill a sink with warm water and dishwashing liquid.

- Submerge the duster head and run your fingers through it to clean.

- Empty the sink and rinse the duster head with clean water.

- Repeat the three steps above until water runs clear.

- Squeeze out excess water and allow to air-dry in the sunshine. Alternatively, if your duster head is machine-washable, wash it in the washing machine.

HOW OFTEN?
Weekly – all surfaces and electrical equipment.
Seasonally – deep clean bookshelves and plants.

To shine and protect wooden furniture, add 2 teaspoons olive oil to Kat's Cleaning Spray and wipe with a dry cleaning cloth.

Easy-to-miss spots

There are lots of areas in the home that can be missed when dusting. Remember that these places collect dust too!

Top of fridge

Top of kitchen cabinets

Ceiling fans

Behind furniture

Under beds

Bedheads

Stair railings

Door frames

Windowsills

Picture frames

THE EXHAUST FAN

The bathroom exhaust fan helps to remove odours and reduce moisture in the air. A dusty filter will reduce its effectiveness, which can in turn lead to mould. For safety, turn off the electricity before cleaning.

KIT

Vacuum cleaner with small brush attachment

Dishwashing liquid

Scrubbing brush

Kat's Cleaning Spray (see page 57) or multi-purpose cleaner

Cleaning cloth

Mini cleaning brush

STEPS

Quick clean

- Use vacuum cleaner with a small brush attachment to remove dust.

Deep clean

- Gently remove the cover. It should be as easy as grabbing the fan cover on either side and gently pulling it down.

- Fill the sink with warm soapy water and soak the cover for 30 minutes. Use a scrubbing brush to clean all parts of the cover. Rinse and set aside to air-dry.

- Spray cleaning spray onto a cloth and carefully wipe away dust build-up on the fan blades. Use a mini cleaning brush for small hard-to-reach areas. Ensure the cover is thoroughly dry before reassembling.

HOW OFTEN?

Seasonally – **quick clean.**

Annually – **deep clean.**

FLOOR RUGS

Floor rugs can make a room feel more cosy and homey, but they can get dirty easily by collecting dust, dirt and hair. Most rugs should come with care labels. Read them to know how to correctly clean your rug.

KIT

Vacuum cleaner

Fresh Carpet Sprinkle (see page 59)

Mop and bucket

STEPS

Quick clean

- Vacuum the top of the rug. To remove smells, lightly sprinkle with the Carpet Sprinkle and sit for 30 minutes, then vacuum to pick up the bicarb soda. Clean vacuum.

Deep clean

- Roll up the rug and move it away from the area to clean. Do not fold as this will cause it to crease. Roll the rug out, upside down. Vacuum the bottom of the rug. Spot clean, as necessary (see pages 78–80).

- Hang or lay the rug outside in the sunlight for a few hours. Giving it a dose of sunshine will naturally disinfect it.

- Vacuum and mop the floor where the rug was sitting to remove any dust and dirt build-up. Put the rug back in place, rotating it 180 degrees to help it wear evenly.

HOW OFTEN?

Weekly – vacuum during regular floor clean.

Annually – deep clean, or more often if you have pets or smokers in the home.

THE FRIDGE

The fridge is one of the hardest-working appliances in our home. It's in use all day, every day. Food and drink can spill onto the shelves though, and if gone unnoticed it will dry up or start to smell, so it's important to give the fridge a regular quick clean. I like to do this before a grocery shop as this is usually the day it is most empty. I also do a quick check of what's in the fridge, meaning I avoid wasting food and buying new ingredients unnecessarily. This also ensures the fridge is clean and tidy before the new food arrives.

When I am about to give my fridge a deep clean, I clear my meal planner. As I empty the fridge and find food or condiments about to expire, I list these at the bottom of my meal planner. I then create a plan based on these ingredients to ensure they are eaten before they spoil. To use up vegetables, I typically make a vegetable slice or beef chow mein for dinner, as these are both filled with plenty of veg. (Go to my website for the recipes.) I don't go a week without meal planning. It helps save my sanity on those busy week-nights, and writing it down on a whiteboard for all the family to see stops the incessant question, 'What's for dinner?'!

KIT

Kat's Reusable Wipes (see page 58), Kat's Cleaning Spray (see page 57) or multi-purpose spray

Cleaning cloths

Dishwashing liquid

Cleaning sponge

Mini cleaning brush

Kat's Sparkle Spray (see page 58) or stainless-steel cleaner, for stainless-steel fridges

Dustpan and brush and broom, for behind the fridge

Mop and bucket, for behind the fridge

STEPS

Quick clean

- Wipe shelves, picking up any food spills or crumbs, using wipes or a cleaning cloth with cleaning spray.

Deep clean

- Empty the fridge. Move all items out of the fridge onto the kitchen bench, or if you feel this task may take you a while, store what you can in an esky. As you put items onto the bench, arrange like items together (such as spreads, condiments, fruit, vegetables).

- Purge expired foods. Throw away food that is out of date or spoiled.

- Clean the shelves. Lay a large towel next to your sink. Fill the sink with warm soapy water. Take all removable parts out of the fridge and wash with a cleaning sponge in the sink. It's important to ensure the water is warm, not hot, as the sudden temperature change on a cold glass shelf may cause it to shatter. Drip dry on a towel.

- Clean inside the fridge. Working from top to bottom, wipe the inside of the fridge with a cloth and cleaning spray. Use a mini brush to remove crumbs from cracks and crevices.

- Clean the door seals. Pay particular attention to the seals, as food and crumbs do get caught in them.

- Reassemble shelves. Dry the shelves and return to the fridge.

- Return the food. Place all food items back in the fridge, wiping over bottoms of jars to remove any sticky spills. As you place items back into the fridge, group similar items together and put nearly expired food to the front as a reminder to use them up.

- Clean the outside of the fridge. Wipe down the outside of the fridge with cleaning spray, paying particular attention to the handles. If your fridge is stainless steel, polish with a paper towel and a splash of olive oil. Wipe in the direction of the grain, adding more oil to the towel when necessary.

To clean behind the fridge

- Unplug your fridge. Slowly pull it away from the wall.

- Clean behind the fridge. Using your dustpan brush or a dry cleaning cloth, wipe away any dust sitting on the back of the fridge, electrical cord and surrounding walls. If dust is stuck on, use the brush attachment on your vacuum cleaner to remove it.

- Clean under the fridge. Use a broom and dustpan to sweep up the dust and dirt under the fridge. Alternatively, you could carefully use your vacuum, but the mess can be sticky and you don't really want that in your vacuum. Mop the floor.

- Move the fridge back into place. Plug it back in and turn on electricity.

 To remove fridge odours, fill an open container with bicarb soda and place it on a bottom shelf to absorb smells.

HOW OFTEN?

Weekly – quick clean.

Seasonally – deep clean.

Annually – behind the fridge.

HARD-SURFACE FLOORS

The floors are the basis of making our homes look tidy – clean floors make the whole home feel fresh. Regularly cleaning the floor keeps it hygienic, as well as preventing scratches, stains and other damage (to other floor areas too). Use a broom or vacuum cleaner to pick up dust and dirt, then mop with a cleaning solution to provide a deep clean.

Select a cleaning solution that is designed for your flooring type: tiles, hard-wood floors or carpet. It is best to follow manufacturer's guidelines because there are many floor types that can't withstand vinegar, lemon juice, oil or too much water. Always spot-test both commercial and DIY cleaners.

For most floor types, you can use hot water. However, when cleaning wooden floors, it's best to use room temperature water as hot water can warp timber. Room temperature water mixed with the right floor cleaner (see page 60) will remove bacteria just as effectively as hot water.

How often you clean your floors will vary between each household. If you have a crawling baby, you will need to clean regularly to pick up all the dirt, grime and germs before their little hands do. Kids running about in the garden or yard will also bring in a lot of dirt. However, if you live alone and work all day, a weekly clean is sufficient.

How to keep floors cleaner for longer

Place doormats at each entry door, for example, front, back, laundry and garage.

If kids come inside from a pool or muddy area, place a towel down for them to dry and wipe their feet on – it's easier to clean a towel than all the floors.

Kids can bring in a lot of dirt on their school socks (such as bark from the playground) so get them to remove school socks before coming inside.

Do a daily quick clean in high-traffic areas.

Wipe up spills as soon as they are made.

Don't wear shoes inside (see page 79).

KIT

Broom or vacuum cleaner

Mop and bucket

Floor Cleaner (see page 60)

Antibacterial cleaner

White vinegar

Mild laundry detergent

STEPS

- Sweep or vacuum the floor to pick up dust and dirt.
- Fill the mop bucket with water and the floor cleaner recommended for your floor type.
- Dip the mop into the bucket and wring the mop to remove as much water as you can. Ensure that the mop is damp, not wet, as this can ruin many floor types and will take too long to dry.
- Work from one end of the room to the other in a side-to-side motion, moving backwards so you are standing on an unmopped area.
- After mopping a small area, rinse the mop head and repeat the process.
- Refill mop bucket with clean water and floor cleaner if needed.
- Allow the floor to dry completely before walking on it.

To clean the mop bucket

- Empty the dirty water from the mop bucket onto the garden or down the drain.
- Rinse the bucket thoroughly with hot water.
- Spray the bucket with vinegar or antibacterial cleaner. Allow the mop bucket to completely dry before storing away.

To clean the mop head

- If the mop head is non-removable, soak in a solution of hot water and 1 cup vinegar for 10 minutes. Wring out and dry in the sunshine.

- If your mop head is machine washable, put it into the washing machine with other dirty cleaning cloths and add 1 cup vinegar with your laundry detergent. Wash and then dry in the sun – the sunlight acts as a natural way to kill bacteria.

 **Kat's tip**

To prevent bacteria growth, never leave your mop head soaking in the bucket longer than 24 hours.

HOW OFTEN?

Daily – quick sweep/vacuum in high-traffic areas (kitchen, front door, living room, under dining table).

Every few days – if you have young children, quick mop regularly crawled areas and toilet.

Weekly – vacuum and mop all floor areas.

THE IRON

If you notice your iron is leaving limescale or rusty water spots on your clothes or not performing well, it needs a good clean to unclog the steam vents or remove marks and water stains. Unplug the iron and ensure it is completely cool before cleaning. Consult the manual for the best advice and to check that vinegar can be used. Avoid tools that will scratch the iron.

KIT

Kat's Cleaning Spray (see page 57)

Cleaning cloths

Dishwashing liquid

White vinegar

Mini brush or cotton tip

STEPS

- Spray cleaning spray onto a cloth and wipe over the iron and soleplate. Alternatively, fill a bowl with warm water and add a few drops of dishwashing liquid. Dip a cloth into the water, then wring out and use to wipe over your iron and soleplate. Wipe with a dry cleaning cloth to remove any water.

- To clean the water reservoir and steam vents, empty water from the iron's reservoir. Refill with ½ cup water and ½ cup vinegar. Stand iron upright on a bench or ironing board with a towel beneath to collect any dirt. Turn iron on, put setting onto high heat and full steam. Let your iron heat for 5 minutes or until water and vinegar evaporate.

- Refill the reservoir with water. Press the steam button and hold for 20 seconds or until the steam flows well, then repeat five times to release dirt and clear the vents. Iron an old rag or tea towel to help remove any debris (better on that than fresh clean clothes!).

- Switch the iron off and allow it to cool before emptying the remaining water from the iron's reservoir. Use a mini brush or cotton tip to gently remove any build-up from the steam vents.

HOW OFTEN?
Seasonally.

Iron soleplate

For stubborn stains and build-up on an iron soleplate
with a non-stick coating, make a paste using
¼ cup bicarb soda and 1 tablespoon white vinegar. Rub
onto the areas with a cloth to pick up the stains. Rinse
with a slightly damp cloth. Wipe clean with a dry
cleaning cloth.

THE KETTLE

Over time the kettle attracts a build-up of limescale. This is a chalky layer that forms over the heating element in the kettle, which then prevents the kettle heating the water to the required temperature. The limescale can also fall away from the element and float in the water, which may then be poured into your next cuppa. To help prevent ants being attracted to your kettle and mineral deposits forming inside, empty the kettle after each use. Ways to use the water: pour boiling water over weeds for natural weed killer, down the sink to kill germs, into the dishwasher filter to clean, over the toilet brush or other cleaning tools to remove bacteria, or once the water has cooled make your own homemade cleaners or water your plants.

KIT

White vinegar

Dish brush

Cleaning cloths

Kat's Cleaning Spray (see page 57), multi-purpose cleaner or Kat's Reusable Wipes (see page 58)

Kat's tip   Instead of using white vinegar to clean your kettle, you can use 1 lemon cut into wedges.

STEPS

- Fill the kettle with 1 part vinegar to 2 parts water. You don't need to fill the entire kettle, just enough to cover the heating element.

- Boil the kettle.

- Allow the water to cool in the kettle for 15 minutes.

- Give it a quick scrub with a dish brush to get all the limescale off.

- Tip out the water and rinse the inside of the kettle with tap water.

- Fill the kettle with water, boil and then empty to remove any lingering cleaning solutions.

- Wipe over the outside of the kettle with a cloth sprayed with cleaner (or use wipes) to remove all dust and dirt, then dry the outside with a dry cloth.

HOW OFTEN?

Monthly.

KITCHEN BENCHTOPS

It may surprise you to know that not every kitchen benchtop can be cleaned with a general multi-purpose cleaner. Acid found in some cleaners can damage some kitchen benchtop surfaces and create dull spots. Instead, each material has different requirements (listed below). As a general rule, avoid abrasive scrubbing pads to keep the integrity of the surface and never place hot saucepans directly onto your benchtop – always use a heat-resistant pot holder.

Each surface has its own unique cleaning solution to help keep it clean. Use any of the following to clean and maintain each surface.

KIT

Marble, quartz, stone or granite

Always clean up spills immediately to avoid staining.

Warm soapy water

Non-abrasive antibacterial cleaner

Kat's Cleaning Spray (see page 57)

Laminate or wooden

Do not use vinegar on your benchtop as this will dull and damage the surface.

Warm soapy water

Non-abrasive antibacterial cleaner

Stainless steel

Warm soapy water

Kat's Sparkle Spray (see page 58) or stainless-steel cleaner

STEPS

Quick clean

- Clean surface with the recommended cleaner and a damp cleaning cloth.

Deep clean

- Remove all items from the kitchen bench, or as you clean, lift items to clean underneath.

- Clean surface with the recommended cleaner and a damp cleaning cloth.

- Clean each item as you place it back onto the kitchen bench to remove grease and dust build-up.

HOW OFTEN?

Daily – quick clean.

Weekly – deep clean.

To help reduce clutter in your kitchen, only keep the appliances that you use regularly on your bench. This will make it easier to clean and a more enticing and manageable area to cook and bake.

KITCHEN CABINETS

Kitchen cabinets can become dirty with dust, food splatters and grease from cooking build-up, which over time becomes sticky. Food drips collect on the tops of drawers and cupboard doors, and crumbs can gather inside drawers and cupboards.

KIT

Dishwashing liquid

Cleaning cloths

Kat's Cleaning Spray (see page 57), degreaser cleaner or Kat's Reusable Wipes (see page 58)

Bicarb soda

White vinegar

Plastic scraper or old credit card

Paper towel

Tea tree oil

Cleaning paste or Lemon Soda Paste (see page 59)

STEPS

Quick clean

- Fill your sink with warm soapy water.

- Wet the cleaning cloth, wring out and work from top cabinets down. Wipe the cupboard doors, drawers and handles, remembering to clean the top of each one to pick up food spills. Rinse the cloth and continue. Alternatively, you can use cleaning spray or reusable wipes.

- Wipe over with a dry cleaning cloth so no watermarks are left behind.

Deep clean

- Spray the tops of your kitchen cabinets with cleaning spray, and sit for 5 minutes. Alternatively, sprinkle with bicarb and spray with vinegar.

- Use a plastic scraper or old credit card to scrape away the oil build-up. Use a paper towel to clean the grease. You don't want to use a cleaning cloth for this as this grease build-up will be hard to remove from your cloth. Repeat the process if necessary. Finally, clean it with cleaning spray and a damp cleaning cloth.

- If you have any sticky residue on your cupboard doors or drawers, dab some tea tree oil onto a cloth and rub over the area. This will penetrate into the grease for easier removal. Allow to sit for a few minutes, then clean the residue away.

- Empty cabinets and drawers, one at a time. Clean with warm soapy water or cleaning spray. For any stubborn marks, use cleaning paste. Wipe over with a dry cleaning cloth so no water is left behind to cause damage. Return items back to cabinets and drawers.

HOW OFTEN?
Weekly – **quick clean.**
Seasonally – **deep clean.**

THE KITCHEN SINK

Between dirty dishes, crumb-filled lunch boxes and hand washing, the kitchen sink can develop a build-up of old food and grime that lingers around the edges and in the sink drain. They are notorious breeding grounds for bacteria, which is why I give my sink a wipe every evening after the dishes are done.

KIT

Kat's Cleaning Spray (see page 57) or antibacterial spray

Cleaning sponge

Mini cleaning brush

Cleaning paste or Lemon Soda Paste (see page 59)

White vinegar

Cleaning cloths

Bicarb soda

Rock salt

Ice

Lemon

STEPS

Quick clean

- Wipe over the sink and tapware with cleaning spray or warm soapy water and a sponge to help avoid dirt and limescale build-up.
- Buff dry with a dry cleaning cloth.

Deep clean

- Remove all dishes and rinse the sink, removing any food and crumbs.

To clean the drain

- Soak the plug in a cup of vinegar for 5 minutes.

- Scrub with a mini brush to remove any build-up.

- Use the mini brush to remove any build-up around the sink drain.

- To help clean and remove odours, sprinkle ½ cup bicarb soda into the drain, then slowly pour in 1 cup vinegar. Sit for 15 minutes. Wash away with boiling water.

To clean the tapware

- Spray tapware with cleaning spray.

- To remove stubborn build-up around tapware and the sink drain, dab on cleaning paste and leave for 10 minutes. If using Lemon Soda Paste, spray with vinegar and leave for a further 5 minutes. Use a mini brush to remove build-up.

- Rinse area with damp cloth.

- Spray again with cleaning spray to remove any lingering paste.

- Polish tapware with a dry cleaning cloth.

To clean the food disposal

- Pour boiling water down the disposal.

- Add ½ cup rock salt and 1 cup ice into your disposal.

- With the water running, turn on your disposal until you can hear that all the salt and ice have been crushed and gone.

- Add ½ cup bicarb soda and sit for 30 minutes.

- Pour in 1 cup vinegar and sit for 15 minutes.

- Turn on the tap and run the disposal.

- Finish by chopping 1 lemon into wedges, add to disposal, then run tap and disposal. The salt and ice will scrub the blades and side of the disposal and the lemon will help to freshen it up.

To clean the sink

- Rinse sink with water.

- Spray sink with cleaning spray and wipe with a cleaning sponge from the top of the sink, working your way down.

- To shine, rub cleaning paste into sink. Alternatively, add some water to Lemon Soda Paste, and use a sponge to wipe runny paste over sink. Leave for 10 minutes. Spray with vinegar and leave for a further 5 minutes. Rub the paste into sink with a sponge.

- Rinse sink with water to remove paste.

- Buff dry with a dry cleaning cloth.

 **Avoid the use of vinegar on concrete, porcelain or cast-iron sinks.**

HOW OFTEN?

Daily – quick clean.

Weekly – deep clean sink and tapware.

Monthly – deep clean drains.

KITCHEN SPLASHBACK

Kitchen splashbacks help to protect the walls from food splatters and they often get covered in grease from cooking. If grease is left too long it can become sticky and harder to remove, so it's best to clean your splashback daily, especially around the stovetop. Splatter should be cleaned immediately so that the splashback does not absorb stains. There are many different types of splashbacks, each requiring a different method of cleaning to avoid scratching or dulling the surface.

KIT

Kat's Cleaning Spray (see page 57), multi-purpose cleaner, degreaser cleaner or Kat's Reusable Wipes (see page 58)

Cleaning cloths

Kat's Sparkle Spray (see page 58), glass cleaner or stainless-steel cleaner

STEPS

Acrylic

- Spray splashback with cleaning spray or use wipes.
- Clean away dirt and grease build-up with a damp cloth. Make sure to clean the grout as well.
- Wipe over with a dry clean cloth to buff.

Tiles

- Spray splashback with cleaning spray or use wipes.
- Clean away dirt and grease build-up with a damp cloth.

Glass

- Spray splashback with Kat's Sparkle Spray or glass cleaner.

- Clean away dirt and grease build-up with a damp cloth.

- Spray splashback again and buff with a dry cleaning cloth.

Stainless steel

- Spray splashback with Kat's Sparkle Spray or stainless-steel cleaner.

- Clean away dirt and grease build-up with a damp cloth.

To polish stainless steel, dab olive oil onto a paper towel and wipe over the splashback following the grain.

HOW OFTEN?

Daily, or immediately for splatter.

KITCHEN SPONGES

Kitchen sponges can become oily and dirty, particularly if you're scrubbing frying pans. Always rinse, wring and hang your sponges and dishcloths to dry after use – never leave them in the bottom of the sink or scrunched up. If left wet, they will become a breeding ground for bacteria, and start to smell. That's certainly not what you want to clean your dishes or benchtops with! If your sponge or cloth has cleaned up raw meat, don't use it again until it has been washed.

Many of us throw sponges away when they get dirty or smelly, but this isn't ideal for our landfill and our future generations. You can easily clean them to remove the bacteria and grime. Once my sponges are not cleaning away any dirt or grease build-up with the quick clean method, it's an indication it's ready for a deeper clean. I rinse the dirty cloth, allow it to air-dry, then add it to my dirty linen pile and wash it in a bulk load in the washing machine, but you can also use your dishwasher.

KIT

White vinegar

Laundry detergent

STEPS

Quick clean

- If the sponge is reasonably clean, rinse under cold water, wring out and allow to air-dry.

- If the sponge needs deep cleaning, rinse and place in the laundry to air-dry before putting it in a basket of dirty cleaning cloths ready for the weekly washing machine deep clean.

Deep clean

- **In the washing machine:** wash in hot water with a small amount of mild laundry detergent and ½ cup vinegar in the fabric softener dispenser. Hang on the line to dry.

- **In the dishwasher:** place your sponge in the top dish rack of your dishwasher and run through a regular wash and drying cycle. Remove from dishwasher, wring out to remove excess water (sponges do not dry well in the dishwasher). Hang on the line to dry.

 **Place your sponge in the sun to dry as sunlight helps to kill bacteria.**

HOW OFTEN?
Daily – quick clean.
Weekly – deep clean.

THE LAUNDRY HAMPER

After dirty laundry sits in the hamper, it can get a little musty and may need a freshen up. To prevent odours, never place damp clothes or towels in the hamper and consider placing a charcoal air-purifying bag in the bottom.

KIT

Cleaning cloth

Kat's Cleaning Spray (see page 57) or multi-purpose cleaner

Dishwashing liquid

Vacuum cleaner with small brush attachment or dustpan brush

STEPS

Plastic

- Wipe with a cleaning cloth and cleaning spray.

Fabric

- Following care instructions, wash in the washing machine. Alternatively, wipe over with a cleaning cloth lightly dampened in warm soapy water. Place on the clothesline to air-dry.

Wooden and wicker

- Using a small brush attachment on a vacuum cleaner or the dustpan brush, brush over the wicker to remove any stuck dirt or dust. Lightly dampen a cleaning cloth in warm soapy water. Wipe over, getting into all cracks and corners. Place the hamper in the sunshine to air-dry before use.

HOW OFTEN?
Monthly.

LIGHT SWITCHES

When we clean, we usually dust surfaces, clean appliances and wash the floors, but often neglect one of the most touched – and grottiest – things … the light switch. Luckily, cleaning light switches only takes a matter of minutes and will leave them fingerprint-, dirt- and germ-free. This is a great task to do while on the phone. To be extra safe, it's a good idea to turn off the power at the outside electricity box.

KIT

Kat's Cleaning Spray (see page 57), multi-purpose cleaner or Kat's Reusable Wipes (see page 58)

Cleaning cloths

Mini cleaning brush

STEPS

- Start at the front of the home, working from left to right and making your way round to each switch plate.
- Lightly spray cleaner onto a cloth and wipe over the switch plate and surrounding wall, removing all dirt, grime and fingerprints. Alternatively, you can use wipes.
- If the switch is dirty, use a mini brush to get into the cracks and crevices.
- Use a dry cleaning cloth to wipe the plate dry.

HOW OFTEN?

Weekly – or daily if there is any illness in the home.

LIGHTING

Lights are magnets for dust, dirt and insects. It's also worth noting that if lights are dirty, they waste more energy. It is best to clean light fixtures in the morning when lights haven't been turned on for at least an hour, as the bulbs can become hot when in use. Remember the Cleaning Cha Cha: clean lighting before the rest of the room, as dust will fall as you work.

A couple of safety notes. Do not use a dripping wet cloth, as you do not want any substance getting into the electrical parts of your lighting – this may damage them and you also risk electrocution. You will need a ladder to reach lighting in the ceiling, so please stay safe and use caution!

KIT

Duster or long-handled duster

Cleaning cloths

Kat's Cleaning Spray (see page 57) or multi-purpose cleaner

 **Add a few drops of lemon essential oil to the cleaning spray to help deter insects.**

STEPS

Quick clean

Lightbulbs
- Gently dust around the bulb with a duster.

Glass ceiling fixtures

- Use a ladder and duster (or long-handled duster) to dust around the top, side and bottom of the light fixtures.

Pendants

- Gently dust the pendant, extension rod and cables with a duster.

Recessed

- Use a duster (or long-handled duster) to dust around the fixture.

Chandelier

- Use a cleaning cloth to very gently dust.

Deep clean

Lightbulbs

- Remove light covers and detach bulb from base. Use a dry cleaning cloth to wipe the bulb clean.

Glass ceiling fixtures

- Fill a sink with warm soapy water and lay a big towel next to the sink. Remove the light fixture from the ceiling. Empty the dust and insects into the bin and clean the fixture with a duster. Place in the sink and soak for 5 minutes. Gently wipe with a cloth, rinse and completely dry with a dry towel. Place light fixture onto the towel next to the sink to finish air-drying. Before reinstalling, clean the lightbulb and dust around the ceiling to remove any dirt, insects and cobwebs.

Pendants

- Dust around the ceiling to remove any dirt, insects and cobwebs. Generously spray cleaner onto a cloth and gently wipe (not too much pressure as you don't want the pendant falling off the ceiling) over the ceiling fixture, cables, extension rod and pendant. Clean the lightbulb.

Recessed

- Remove the bulb and dust inside the fixture. If needed, lightly spray cleaner onto a dry cloth and clean, avoiding the bulb outlet. Buff dry with a dry cleaning cloth. Clean the lightbulb and put it back into place.

Chandelier

- Remove the chandelier if easier. Spray the cleaner onto a cloth and gently wipe over each piece of the chandelier. Finish by wiping over again with a clean dry cloth to buff and shine. Use a dry cleaning cloth to clean the dust off the bulb.

HOW OFTEN?

Weekly or monthly – **quick clean.**

Seasonally – **deep clean.**

Cleaning fabric lampshades

Cleaning a lampshade is a delicate process. Remove the shade from the base. Use a duster or a vacuum cleaner with a brush attachment to remove dust from the shade. Alternatively, you could use a silicone glove or lint roller.

MAKEUP BRUSHES

Between all the contouring, highlighting, blush and foundation application, our makeup brushes can build up dirt and oils. This can cause bacteria growth, which may lead to acne breakouts and other skin concerns. Regular cleaning of your makeup brushes can extend their lifespan. I use a dedicated kitchen sponge to clean my brushes. Alternatively, for a gentler approach, you could use a makeup cleaning pad. When cleaning your brushes, avoid getting water above the handle of the brush as this may affect the glue holding the bristles in place.

KIT

Makeup cleaning pad or cleaning sponge

Gentle shampoo

STEPS

- Rinse the brush bristles under running water, being sure to angle them down so you are not damaging the base of the bristles.
- Dampen the cleaning pad or sponge with warm water and squeeze a few drops of gentle shampoo onto it.
- Gently swirl your brushes in the shampoo, changing direction every so often and gently massaging the bristles to remove any makeup and oil build-up.
- Rinse your brushes under running water. Repeat the steps above if the water doesn't run clean.
- Gently squeeze out any excess water and re-shape the brush to its original shape.
- Lay flat to completely dry.

HOW OFTEN?

Weekly.

MATTRESSES

While we sleep our bodies shed sweat, oil and dead skin cells, which linger on the sheets, settle into the mattress and can leave yellow stains. Make the process of cleaning your mattress easier by using a mattress protector, which can easily be removed and cleaned in the washing machine. A mattress protector creates a barrier between your sheets and the mattress, reducing the impact of sweat, skin cells and 'wet spots'. With regular cleaning of your mattress protector it can also help relieve the symptoms of dust mite aller-gies. And it goes without saying that getting a waterproof mattress protector will save your sanity during toilet training stages!

KIT
Bicarb soda

Vacuum cleaner with upholstery tool

Cleaning cloths

Kat's Cleaning Spray (see page 57) or fabric upholstery cleaner

Kat's Mattress Spray (see page 61)

STEPS
- Remove all linens from the bed and wash.
- Open the windows in the room to let in the fresh air.

Quick freshen up
- Sprinkle bicarb soda over the mattress to absorb sweat and odours, sit for 30 minutes, then vacuum. Remember to empty and clean your vacuum immediately.

Toilet training accidents
- Clean the area immediately to prevent bacteria and smells from

settling in. Lightly spray stains with the cleaner. Use a dry cloth and gently dab the area to absorb as much moisture as you can. Sprinkle bicarb soda over the affected area to absorb any remaining moisture and odour, then leave for 6–8 hours (the longer the better). Vacuum the mattress to pick up the bicarb. Clean the vacuum to remove any bicarb build-up or smells. If you can, move the mattress out into direct sunlight as it can help sanitise and freshen the mattress naturally.

Stains

- Lightly spray stains with cleaner, dabbing with a cloth until the stain lifts. Do not rub the mattress. If needed, use another dry cloth, again dabbing the area repeatedly to lift as much water as possible. Do not leave the area too damp as this may cause a water stain. Allow the area to dry thoroughly.

Deep clean

- Sprinkle bicarb soda over the mattress to absorb sweat and odours, let sit for 30 minutes, then vacuum. Remember to empty and clean your vacuum immediately.

- Vacuum the top and sides of the mattress using an upholstery tool. Use the crevice tool to get into the seamed edges.

- Spray mattress spray onto the bed. This will help absorb odours, deter dust mites and leave the mattress smelling fresh.

- Leave the mattress as long as you can to absorb the spray and air-dry.

- Make the bed – not forgetting your mattress protector!

HOW OFTEN?

Immediately – **toilet training accidents and stains.**

Monthly – **deep clean the mattress and wash the mattress protector.**

THE MICROWAVE

It doesn't take too much for the microwave to become a mess – reheating spaghetti bolognese comes to mind! – but ignoring these food splatters can actually increase cooking times. Food smells can linger too, so this method helps both clean and freshen. Never use abrasive cleaners in your microwave as this may cause damage.

KIT

White vinegar

Cleaning sponge

Dishwashing liquid

Cleaning cloths

Mini brush

Kat's Cleaning Spray (see page 57), multi-purpose cleaner or Kat's Reusable Wipes (see page 58)

STEPS

Quick clean

- Fill a microwave-safe jug with 1 cup water and 2 tablespoons vinegar.

- Place the jug in the microwave and turn it on High for 5 minutes.

- Let sit for 5 minutes to allow the steam to loosen any food residue.

- Open the door and remove the jug. Wipe the inside walls and turntable with a sponge. Wipe along the keypad and front of the door to finish.

 You can replace the white vinegar with 1 lemon cut into quarters.

Deep clean

- Clean the inside of the microwave, following the quick clean steps opposite.

- Fill the kitchen sink with warm soapy water.

- Remove the glass turntable and place it in the sink to soak.

- Unplug and remove the microwave from the shelf.

- Wipe the electrical cord with a dry cloth, removing all dust particles.

- Dip the cloth in water, rinse and wring out. Use the cloth to clean the exterior of the microwave.

- Use a mini brush to remove any crumbs or build-up in cracks or crevices.

- Clean the shelf with spray or wipes to remove dust and crumbs. Return the microwave to shelf.

- Clean the turntable, dry and place it back into the microwave.

HOW OFTEN?

Weekly – quick clean.

Monthly – deep clean.

MIRRORS

Fingerprints, toothpaste splatter and streaks on a dirty mirror can be unsightly. If you have stubborn streaks, you can use white vinegar to remove the build-up on the glass, before following the steps below. Remember to spray and wipe quickly (don't spray and walk away) to avoid dirtying the mirror further with water stains.

KIT

Lint-free cleaning cloths

Kat's Sparkle Spray (see page 58) or glass cleaner

STEPS

- Use a dry cleaning cloth to wipe over the mirror and pick up any dust from the surface.
- Lightly spray Kat's Sparkle Spray or glass cleaner all over the mirror.
- Fold your cloth in quarters and wipe the mirror from top to bottom in a zigzag motion.
- Fold your cloth over to use a clean and dry quarter and wipe again to buff.
- Stand back and check that you have picked up all the dirt and dust.

Kat's tip

Are you constantly wiping your foggy mirror after a shower? There is an easy fix! Cover your mirror with a cheap foam-based shaving cream, leave it for 30 seconds and buff the shaving cream into the mirror with a cleaning cloth until it has all gone.

HOW OFTEN?
Weekly.

THE OVEN

Cleaning the oven is definitely one of my least favourite jobs to do. However, I love to bake and a clean oven makes the experience much more enjoyable. I try to prevent mess by placing pie and casserole dishes on a baking tray so I can clean any spills from the tray rather than having to scrub the oven. I have to admit that as much as I love using natural cleaning products, there are particular food spills that I cannot remove naturally – at times like these I do need to use oven cleaner to help remove those extra stubborn baked-on spots.

KIT

Kat's Cleaning Spray (see page 57) or multi-purpose cleaner

Cleaning sponge

Cleaning paste or Lemon Soda Paste (see page 59) with a few drops of dishwashing liquid

White vinegar

Cleaning cloths

Kat's Sparkle Spray (see page 58) or stainless-steel cleaner

Oxi powder stain remover

Oven cleaner

Gloves

Grill cleaning brush

STEPS

Quick clean

- Using cleaning spray and sponge, clean the oven's interior and internal door to remove any grease and grime.

- For stubborn marks, dab cleaning paste onto the area, sit for 5 minutes, then remove with a damp cleaning sponge. Alternatively, add a few drops of dishwashing liquid to Lemon Soda Paste and apply to the area; after 10 minutes, spritz with vinegar and sit for 5 minutes. Gently clean the area, then clean again with spray and a cloth to remove paste residue.

- Clean the exterior door with cleaning spray and a cloth. If your oven is stainless steel, use a paper towel with a splash of olive oil. Wipe in the direction of the grain, adding more oil to the towel when necessary.

Deep clean

- Soak the oven shelves and side racks. Place an old towel or a sheet in your bathtub to help prevent scratching the tub. Remove the shelves and side rails from your oven and place on top of the towel. Sprinkle ¾ cup oxi powder stain remover over the top. Fill the bath with hot water, enough to cover the shelves. Leave for a few hours or overnight to help loosen the grime.

- Remove baked-on food on the bottom of the oven. If your oven has a self-clean setting, run this to help make the cleaning process easier. Once the oven is switched off and cooled down, clean with cleaning spray and a sponge. For baked-on grime, dab cleaning paste onto the area, sit for 5 minutes, then remove with a damp cleaning sponge. For stubborn stains that will not clean away with previous method, use oven cleaner.

- Clean the oven door. Spread cleaning paste over the oven door, stand for 30 minutes, then use a damp cleaning sponge to remove the grime. Alternatively, add a few drops of dishwashing liquid to Lemon Soda Paste and apply to the area; after 10 minutes, spritz with vinegar and sit for 5 minutes. Gently clean the area, then clean again with spray and a cloth to remove paste residue.

- One last wipe over. Spray the oven interior and door with cleaning spray to wipe away any leftover paste. Rinse the cloth and wipe again to reveal your sparkling clean oven and door.

- Clean the oven shelves. After the shelves have been soaking overnight, put on some gloves and gently scrub the shelves with a cleaning sponge or grill cleaning brush. Empty the bathtub. Fill a bucket up with water and pour over the shelves to rinse off, then allow to dry.

- Replace the oven racks. Place your racks and shelves back in your beautifully clean oven.

- Clean the exterior of your oven. Use cleaning spray and a cleaning cloth to clean marks and fingerprints. If your oven is stainless steel, use a paper towel with a splash of olive oil and wipe in the direction of the grain, adding more oil to the towel when necessary.

HOW OFTEN?
Daily – spot clean.
Weekly – quick clean.
Seasonally – deep clean.

THE PANTRY

Dust, grease, grime and sticky spots can all occur in the pantry. It's important to give it a regular clean to keep away pests and bugs. That said, no matter how clean your kitchen is, pantry bugs can appear. The most common pantry bugs are moths, weevils and ants. Weevils find their way into the home in the food we buy from the grocery store, such as flour, rice, grains and cereals. Do a regular check to make sure you don't have an infestation in your food.

KIT

Kat's Cleaning Spray (see page 57), multi-purpose cleaner or Kat's Reusable Wipes (see page 58)

Cleaning cloths

Cleaning paste or Lemon Soda Paste (see page 59)

White vinegar

STEPS

Quick clean

- Tidy the pantry by putting all items back into their correct place.

- Without removing any items, spray the cleaner onto a cleaning cloth, or use wipes, and wipe down the visible shelving.

- Pay particular attention to the shelves or containers that store your sauces, oils, salt/pepper and honey, as you may find this area easily becomes messy and sticky.

Deep clean

- Remove all items from the pantry, grouping like items together and glancing at expiry dates as you do so. Throw away any food items that have expired.

- Spray the shelf with cleaner, or use wipes, and wipe over with a cloth.

- For stubborn marks, dab on cleaning paste using a cloth, sit for 5 minutes, then gently clean area. Alternatively, apply Lemon Soda Paste, sit for 10 minutes, then spritz with vinegar, sit for 5 minutes and gently clean area. Clean again to remove paste residue with cleaning spray and a cloth.

- Place items back into the pantry organising them into categories (that is a whole other book!), wiping the containers with a cloth as you do so.

HOW OFTEN?
Weekly – quick clean.
Seasonally – deep clean.

If you have pantry bugs, add ½ cup white vinegar, ½ cup water and 8 drops each of lavender, peppermint, eucalyptus and clove essential oils to a spray bottle. Spray onto the cleaned pantry surface to help keep the pantry bugs away naturally.

PILLOWS

Dirty pillows can contribute to lost sleep and heightened allergies from the dead skin, bugs, proteins in the waste and decomposed dust mites. They also collect sweat, drool, germs, dust and dirt … When you consider we lay our head on this every night, it's clear they deserve a little attention.

Clean your pillows on a sunny day as you want them to dry as quickly as possible in the sunshine. Always check the tags first to make sure they can be washed in the washing machine.

Finally, use pillow protectors to reduce the times you need to regularly clean the pillow. They help to stop makeup, sweat, hair products and drool getting into your pillow. Read care instructions on the label to follow the best cleaning method and water temperature. Feather pillows should not be washed – follow the no-wash steps to refresh your pillow.

KIT

Mild laundry detergent

White vinegar

Tea tree essential oil

Bicarb soda

Vacuum cleaner with small brush attachment

Laundry Stripping Mix (see page 61)

STEPS

- Remove the pillowcase and pillow protector (see page 72 for steps to wash pillow protector).
- Always wash two pillows together in the washing machine to help balance the load.

Top loader washing machine

- Set the washing machine to the longest gentle/delicate cycle and fill with warm water.

- As it's filling, add half the detergent you would normally use. Don't use too much, as it can stick to and damage the pillow's fibres.

- Use ½ cup vinegar and 10 drops of tea tree oil instead of fabric softener.

- Once the detergent has dissolved, place the pillows in the washing machine, submerging them in the water. Leave the lid of the machine open for 1–2 hours to allow the pillows to soak.

- Close the lid and let the machine run through its full cycle.

- Repeat the rinse cycle to ensure all detergent is washed away.

Front loader washing machine

- Place the pillows in the washing machine.

- Add half the detergent you would normally use to the detergent dispenser. Don't use too much, as it can stick to and damage the pillow's fibres.

- Use ½ cup vinegar and 10 drops of tea tree oil instead of fabric softener.

- Wash on a warm temperature gentle/delicate cycle.

- Repeat the rinse cycle to ensure all the detergent is washed away.

No-wash freshen up

- Sprinkle the pillows with bicarb soda and let it sit for an hour.

- Use the small brush attachment on the vacuum to vacuum up the bicarb.

- Shake the pillow well to remove any bicarb.

- Lay the pillows over the clothesline in the sunshine for several hours.

Deep soak

- Fill the bathtub with hot water. Sprinkle in the Laundry Stripping Mix and stir to dissolve.

- Submerge the pillows in the water and soak for at least 4 hours or overnight. Stir the water occasionally.

- Drain the bathtub and squeeze as much water as you can from the pillows.

- Line a washing basket with a towel and place the pillows in basket. The towel will help absorb any drips, rather than dripping from the bathroom to the laundry.

- Put the pillows into your washing machine, add ½ cup vinegar in the fabric softener dispenser and run through a rinse and spin cycle.

- Repeat the cycle to ensure all the detergent is washed away.

Drying pillows

- Lay the pillows over the clothesline to help air circulate around them and allow the sunshine to help destroy allergens and dust mites.

HOW OFTEN?

Seasonally.

Add a spritz of your favourite pillow or linen spray to your pillows each morning to freshen or in the evening to help promote restful sleep.

QUILT COVERS AND INSERTS

A quilt cover not only helps decorate a bedroom, but it helps to protect the quilt insert from sweat and dust mites, minimising the impact of moisture and bacteria build-up. Most quilt inserts can be machine washed (check care instructions on the label), although they may be too big for your washing machine. If you really need to push a quilt in, it's best to wash it by hand. Ensure it has enough space to move around so water and detergent wash it thoroughly. Wash wool inserts on wool cycle in the washing machine. Handwash feather inserts. Alternatively, you can get your insert dry-cleaned or visit your local laundry mat – it's a good idea to look up reviews first so you can be sure the machines are clean.

To reduce the need to wash your quilt cover and insert more regularly, fold your bed sheet over the top of your quilt so your face and armpits are touching the sheets rather than the quilt.

KIT

Laundry detergent

White vinegar

Essential oil

Wool dryer balls

STEPS

Machine wash

- Separate quilt cover and insert.

- Wash cover and insert on a gentle cycle in the washing machine, at a temperature recommended on care instruction label. Do not use too much laundry detergent as it can damage the quilt's fibres.

- Use ½ cup vinegar and a few drops of your favourite essential oil instead of fabric softener.

- Remove from the washing machine and shake to loosen up any clumps.

- Dry in the sun on the clothesline, as the sunlight acts as a natural way to remove odours and kill bacteria. Drying may take some time. Alternatively, if care instructions advise your quilt can be tumble dried and it fits in the dryer, dry at low temperature with wool dryer balls to help the air circulate.

- Stretch the quilt insert out and over a number of lines to help the air circulate around it, then secure with pegs.

Handwash

- Do this early in the morning to allow enough time for the quilt insert to dry.

- Half-fill the bathtub with warm water and a few drops of laundry detergent.

- Place the insert in the tub, squeezing the water through it; if the water gets too dirty, drain and repeat.

- Soak for an hour, or overnight if you are drying tomorrow.

- Drain the bathtub and refill with cold water.

- Squeeze water through the insert to rinse. Drain the bathtub.

- Repeat until all the detergent is gone and the water runs clear.

- Roll the quilt insert while in the tub to remove the excess water before lifting it out of the tub. Alternatively, with clean feet, stand on top and squish more water out. Try and remove as much water as you can as this will help with the drying process.

- Get the biggest towel you can find. Wrap the insert in the towel to help absorb any drips. Place the insert in a washing basket and take the insert to the line or dryer.

Drying

- Shake the insert to loosen up any clumps.

- Dry in the sun on the clothesline, as the sunlight acts as a natural way to remove odours and kill bacteria. Drying your insert may take some time. Alternatively, if care instructions advise your insert can be tumble dried and it fits in the dryer, dry on low temperature with wool dryer balls to help the air circulate.

- Stretch the quilt cover out and over a number of lines to help the air circulate around it, then secure with pegs.

HOW OFTEN?

Weekly – if a regular flat sheet is not used or if pets sleep on your quilt.

Monthly – quilt cover and place insert out in the sun to air.

Seasonally – quilt insert.

Laundry stripping

If your laundry needs a deep clean, you may want to try the popular trend of laundry stripping. The combination of cleaners helps remove the build-up of dirt, laundry detergent, fabric softener, body oils and stains. Deep soaking non-colourfast items such as quilts, blankets, pillows, towels or kitchen linens overnight aims to remove residue, brighten textiles and improve their condition. Use the bathtub as you'll have more room to soak. Beware it can be quite mortifying to see the amount of dirt that comes out of an item that looks reasonably clean! Follow the deep soak tips on pages 156–7 and find the Laundry Stripping Mix on page 61.

THE RANGEHOOD

The purpose of the stove rangehood is to collect fumes and grease from your cooking, so you can only imagine how much grime it catches. Keeping the filter clean improves power efficiency and allows the rangehood to work effectively.

KIT

Kat's Cleaning Spray (see page 57) or degreaser cleaner

Cleaning cloths

Kat's Sparkle Spray (see page 58) or stainless-steel cleaner

Bicarb soda

Dishwashing liquid

Dish brush

STEPS

Quick clean

- Use cleaning spray and a cleaning cloth to clean away dust, grease and grime build-up on the rangehood.
- If your rangehood is stainless steel, polish with Kat's Sparkle Spray or stainless-steel cleaner.

Deep clean

- Fill a sink with boiling water. Add ¼ cup bicarb soda and 2 tablespoons dishwashing liquid and carefully mix with dish brush.
- Remove the filters from the rangehood and place them in the sink, covering them with hot water. Soak the filters for 15 minutes.
- If your sink water is filthy, empty the sink and refill with clean water, adding dishwashing liquid.

- Use a dish brush to scrub the filters to remove any trapped grease.
- Rinse the filters thoroughly in hot water to remove dishwashing liquid and grease.
- Air-dry before placing filters back in the rangehood.
- Spray with cleaning spray and wipe over the rest of the rangehood with a cleaning cloth to remove grease and dust build-up.

 **Newer rangehood filters can be placed in the dishwasher to clean – check your manual for instructions.**

HOW OFTEN?

Weekly – quick clean.

Monthly – deep clean.

REMOTE CONTROLS

Remote controls are touched by everybody in the home: in our home, even the cat tends to sit on it! As a result, they get a build-up of dust, dirt and germs over time, so it's a good idea to regularly clean them. The task shouldn't take any longer than 5 minutes, so you can do it during an ad break while watching TV in the evening. You do need to take care when cleaning your remotes as you don't want to damage the buttons or batteries. Check to see if your manual includes instructions on how to clean the remote control; otherwise follow these steps below.

KIT

Cleaning cloth

Kat's Cleaning Spray (see page 57), multi-purpose cleaner or Kat's Reusable Wipes (see page 58)

Cotton bud or toothpick

STEPS

- Remove the batteries.
- Spray a cleaning cloth with cleaning spray or use your homemade cleaning wipes. Wipe over the remote.
- If there is a build-up of dirt, use a cotton tip or toothpick to remove it. Be careful not to break the toothpick as this may damage the remote.
- Put the batteries back in.

HOW OFTEN?
Weekly.

RUBBER BATH TOYS

Rubber duckies are popular bath toys. However, being that they are submerged in warm water, they can develop a horrible build-up of bacteria and mould inside. Alternatively, you could seal the hole in the bath toy with hot glue.

KIT

White vinegar

Cleaning cloth

Mini brush

STEPS

Quick clean

- Rinse bath toys and squeeze out all water after use. Wipe dry and place in a dry spot with the squeeze hole up to help them dry inside before the next bath.

Deep clean

- Squeeze out any water sitting inside the toys.
- Fill the bathroom sink with water, add 1 cup vinegar and mix.
- Use a cleaning cloth to clean the outside of the toys.
- Suck water into each rubber toy and allow to soak for 15 minutes. Shake and sit for a further 15 minutes. Shake again and squeeze out build-up and water.
- Using a cloth or mini brush, clean each toy. Rinse and allow to air-dry.

HOW OFTEN?

Daily – **quick clean.**

Weekly – **deep clean.**

RUBBISH BINS

Rubbish bins are a breeding ground for bacteria. It's essential to keep them clean to ensure you have a healthy kitchen. Bins with pedals or sensors are ideal to minimise touching of the bin (and germs). Empty the bin frequently to avoid moisture build-up and prevent mould. Avoid tears and unnecessary spills, by using good-quality bin bags that are the same size as the bin: simple but effective!

KIT

Kat's Cleaning Spray (see page 57) or antibacterial spray

Paper towel

Dishwashing liquid

Scrubbing brush

White vinegar

STEPS

Quick clean

- When the bin is empty, spritz entire lid and bottom of the inside of the bin with cleaning spray.

- Sit for 5 minutes.

- Use a paper towel and more cleaning spray to clean base and lid.

- Add a new bin liner.

Deep clean

- Take the bin outside and rinse with a garden hose. Alternatively, clean in the laundry sink.

- Fill the bin slightly with water.

- Add a few drops of dishwashing liquid and clean the base and lid with a scrubbing brush.

- Empty water from the bin and rinse with clean water.

- Spray the base and lid with vinegar. Dry in the sunshine.

- Disinfect the scrubbing brush by pouring boiling water over it, then soak bristles in vinegar for an hour. Rinse, shake and then air-dry.

HOW OFTEN?

Weekly – quick clean.

Monthly – deep clean.

Bicarb soda (or Fresh Carpet Sprinkle; see page 60) sprinkled into the base of the bin will help absorb moisture and smells.

THE SHOWER

All the dirt from our bodies falls onto the surface of the shower, which attracts mildew, bacteria and grime. You may even find your showerhead squirting water at all angles if it is blocked. When you're cleaning the shower, open the bathroom windows to help with ventilation. I get asked a lot, 'When is the best time to clean the shower?' I get in the shower, run the water, put on a body scrub, or wet my hair and add in a leave-in conditioner. Then I turn off the water, clean the shower and finish my shower routine. As the surface is already wet and the steam hits the shower walls, it makes this task that little bit easier, and I have beautifully soft skin or hair afterwards. The kids have their own shower, which they now mostly clean themselves. On the occasions I clean it, I go in fully clothed (activewear is best) and scrub it just after they have finished showering.

KIT

Cleaning cloths

Dishwashing liquid

Kat's Mould Be Gone Spray (see page 57) or mould remover

Grout cleaning brush

Kat's Cleaning Spray (see page 57) or bathroom cleaner

Cleaning sponge

Cleaning paste or Lemon Soda Paste (see page 59)

Scrubbing brush or broom

Mini cleaning brush

White vinegar

Bicarb soda

Toothpick

STEPS

- Empty the shower of all contents. Wipe over each item with a cleaning cloth dipped in warm soapy water to remove any soap build-up.

- Deal with any mould. Spray Mould Be Gone Spray or mould remover onto visible mould patches. After 5 minutes, use the grout cleaning brush to remove. Rinse area.

Glass, walls, floors and tapware

- Spray cleaning spray on the glass, walls and floor of the shower. Use a cleaning sponge to clean the glass. Use a sponge or scrubbing brush to clean the walls and floor. Alternatively, you could use a broom to scrub these areas if you have trouble bending.

- To remove stubborn build-up around tapware, dab on cleaning paste and leave for 10 minutes. If using Lemon Soda Paste, spray with vinegar and leave for a further 5 minutes. Use a mini brush to remove build-up. Rinse with a damp cloth.

- Rinse the glass, walls and floor from top to bottom with water using the showerhead or bucket filled with water. To prevent water spots, use a squeegee to remove any water from the surface.

Shower door seal

- Fill the bathroom sink with soapy water. Remove the rubber seal from the bottom of the shower door; it should slip off quite easily.

- Dip a mini brush or cleaning cloth into the soapy water and clean the seal.

- Spritz a dry cloth with vinegar and wipe over the seal.

- Wait until the seal is completely dry before putting back into place.

Shower drain

- Add a squirt of dishwashing liquid down the drain. Sprinkle in 1 cup bicarb soda and pour in 1 cup vinegar.

- Allow to sit for 5 minutes. If using Lemon Soda Paste, spritz with vinegar and sit for a further 5 minutes, then pour boiling water down the drain. This method should effectively clear away most of the hair clogging up the drain. Alternatively, if your drain has a removable cover, you can remove hair by hand.

Showerhead

- Dab cleaning paste over the showerhead and sit for 5 minutes. If using Lemon Soda Paste, spritz with vinegar and sit for a further 5 minutes. Scrub with a mini brush to remove debris. Rinse.

- Half-fill a bag (or bucket if the showerhead is detachable) with vinegar. Insert the showerhead in the bag, immersing it in the vinegar. Tie the bag with a rubber band to secure onto showerhead and sit overnight (if you have a brass or gold showerhead, remove after 30 minutes).

- Remove the showerhead from the bag and use the mini brush to clean build-up. Turn on the water to flush out any mineral deposits. Use a toothpick to poke the holes to help remove mineral deposits, if needed. Rinse with water.

- Polish the showerhead with a dry cleaning cloth.

Need to fix a rust ring? Use a cleaning cloth with cleaning paste, dab onto the spot, sit for 2 minutes, then wipe away. Alternatively, cover the stain with lemon juice and a sprinkle of salt and soak for 3–4 hours. Use a cleaning cloth to gently scrub the area.

HOW OFTEN?

Weekly – mould; glass, walls, floor and tapware.

Monthly – shower door seal; shower drain.

Seasonally – showerhead.

SKIRTING BOARDS

It's easy to overlook our skirting boards when we're cleaning the home, but just like with our furniture and floors, dust accumulates here too. Don't clean skirting boards with your mop as this will result in dust sticking to the boards, making them harder to clean. To avoid bending down, you can use a broom or stick vacuum with a long handle and brush attachment.

KIT

Duster, dustpan brush or vacuum cleaner with brush attachment

Cleaning cloth

Kat's Cleaning Spray (see page 57), multi-purpose cleaner or Kat's Reusable Wipes (see page 58)

Mini cleaning brush

Melamine foam

STEPS

- Dust the skirting boards using a duster, dustpan brush or the brush attachment on your vacuum cleaner.
- For stubborn dirt build-up (often around the fridge or washing machine), spot clean using a damp cleaning cloth and spray, or wipes.
- Use the mini cleaning brush to help remove dust from tight corners or decorative folds.
- Remove scuff marks by using the melamine foam.

HOW OFTEN?

Seasonally – or you may need to clean more often if you live in an area with dust stirring regularly outside.

STAINLESS-STEEL APPLIANCES

Water stains, dust and fingerprints can mark the surface of most stainless-steel appliances. If left, this can cause the surface to rust.

KIT

Cleaning cloths

Duster

Kat's Sparkle Spray (see page 58) or stainless-steel cleaner

Paper towel

Olive oil

STEPS

- Use a dry cleaning cloth or duster to remove dust and hair.

- Spray with Kat's Sparkle Spray or stainless-steel cleaner and wipe over with a cloth to remove all dirt and grime build-up.

- Polish away the fingerprints using a paper towel with a splash of olive oil. Wipe in the direction of the grain, adding more oil to the towel when necessary.

- Finish with a dry cleaning cloth to wipe away any excess oil.

HOW OFTEN?
Weekly.

THE STOVETOP

Spills and splatters are inevitable when cooking on the stovetop. For the most part, they can be easily wiped away if cleaned up immediately. But it's the burnt-on food that may require some extra attention. Always ensure your cooktop is cool before you start to clean and follow your manufacturer's instructions.

KIT

Kat's Cleaning Spray (see page 57), degreaser cleaner or Kat's Reusable Wipes (see page 58)

Cleaning cloths

Mini cleaning brush or toothpick

Cleaning sponge

Bicarb soda

Dishwashing liquid

Cooktop scraper (optional)

Cleaning paste or Lemon Soda Paste (see page 59)

White vinegar

STEPS

Quick clean

Glass cooktop

- Spray the surface with cleaning spray and wipe with a damp cloth (or use wipes) to remove any splatters and spills.
- Use a mini cleaning brush or toothpick to remove crumbs stuck between the edges of your cooktop and bench.

Gas cooktop

- When cool, pick up the grates, spray the surface with cleaning spray and use a damp cloth to remove any splatters and spills. Wipe over the grates with the cloth as you place them back.

Electric cooktop

- Use a lightly dampened cloth dipped in hot water and dishwashing liquid to wipe over coil or plate burners.

- For stubborn grime, apply cleaning paste. Alternatively, apply Lemon Soda Paste, allow to sit for 10 minutes, then spritz with vinegar, sit for another 5 minutes and then gently clean area. Clean again to remove paste residue with cleaning spray and a cloth.

- Spray the entire cooktop with cleaning spray and polish dry with a cloth.

Deep clean

Glass cooktop

- Spray the cooktop with cleaning spray. Remove splatters and spills with a damp cleaning sponge.

- For burnt-on food, sprinkle the area with bicarb soda. Lay a lightly wrung-out cleaning cloth that has been soaked in hot water and dishwashing liquid over the baked-on area. Leave for 30 minutes, then use the cloth to wipe away build-up. You can also use a cooktop scraper, carefully following instructions to gently scrape off the burnt food. Wipe the cooktop with a cloth and repeat until removed.

- For stubborn marks, apply a small amount of cleaning paste directly onto the mark and allow to sit for 5 minutes. Use a cleaning sponge or cloth to buff the area until the mark has disappeared. Repeat if necessary. Alternatively, add a few drops of water to Lemon Soda Paste and wipe over the cooktop with a cloth. Leave for 10 minutes. Spray with vinegar and leave for a further 5 minutes. Wipe over with a damp cloth. Buff dry with a dry cleaning cloth.

- Spray the entire cooktop with cleaning spray and polish dry with a cloth.

Gas cooktop

- Fill the sink with hot water and add a few drops of dishwashing liquid.

- Place grates and burner heads in the sink (use the laundry tub if the sink is too small, placing a towel in the bottom of the sink to prevent scratches) and soak for 30 minutes. Use a cleaning sponge to clean away grease build-up. Rinse and lay on a towel to dry. Check your cooktop manual first as some grates may be placed in the dishwasher for an easy clean.

- Spray cleaning spray onto a cleaning cloth and clean inside the burners, picking up any spills. Use cleaning paste or Lemon Soda Paste for stubborn marks around the burners and a mini cleaning brush to remove crumbs. Use a damp cloth to remove the paste and wipe away crumbs.

- Spray the entire cooktop with cleaning spray and polish dry with a cleaning cloth.

- Place the completely dry grates and burner heads back.

HOW OFTEN?

Daily – quick clean after every use.

Monthly – deep clean.

THROW BLANKETS

Throw blankets are used as decoration or for snuggling up when it's cold. Pets, food, drinks, hair, body oils and dust can make them less than clean. Always check care instructions before cleaning. Spot clean knit throws.

KIT

Mild laundry detergent

White vinegar

STEPS

• Wash the throw by itself in the washing machine on a cold delicate cycle with mild laundry detergent and ½ cup vinegar and a few drops of your favourite essential oil in the fabric softener dispenser. Don't use too much detergent.

• Air-dry on the clothesline in the sun.

HOW OFTEN?

Monthly – or more often if used by pets.

THE TOILET

Not the most appealing of tasks, but regular cleaning will remove smells, bacteria, stains and mineral build-up to give you a sparkling porcelain throne. I am a huge fan of reusable cloths, but in the instance of cleaning a toilet, my personal preference is paper towel or toilet paper. Place paper towels in the bin (do not flush down the toilet). If you use gloves while you clean your toilet, clean them with antibacterial cleaner and leave to air-dry.

If you live in an area with hard water, your toilets can build up mineral deposits, such as calcium, magnesium and lime. This build-up of minerals or hard water scale leaves an unsightly permanent brown stain at the bottom of the toilet bowl that you just can't get rid of, no matter how much you clean the toilet. I have found a product called Bar Keepers Friend Toilet Bowl Cleaner which works absolute wonders at lifting the stain. No more embarrassing brown stains in the bowl of your loo!

KIT

Toilet cleaner

Kat's Cleaning Spray (see page 57) or antibacterial cleaner

Paper towel or eco-friendly antibacterial wipes

Gloves

Bar Keepers Friend Toilet Bowl Cleaner

Lemon Soda Paste (see page 59) or cleaning paste

White vinegar

STEPS

Quick clean

- Flush the toilet. Apply toilet cleaner to the bowl and around the rim, close the lid and leave to soak.

- Meanwhile, spray Kat's Cleaning Spray or antibacterial cleaner all over the exterior of the toilet including the toilet button/flush. Don't forget the base of the toilet, or the floor and walls behind and to the side of the toilet. Leave for 5 minutes.

- Working from top to bottom (tank, button, lid, exterior of the toilet bowl, back of the toilet bowl), clean with paper towel or wipes.

- Spray under the lid, toilet seat and under the toilet seat with cleaner, then wipe clean with paper towel or toilet paper.

- Remove the toilet brush from its holder, add a splash of vinegar to the brush holder. Use the toilet brush to clean inside the bowl, starting around the rim, then around the bowl, top to bottom, and the drain hole. Swish vinegar in holder, then empty into toilet.

- Flush the toilet, placing the brush under the running water to rinse. Place the brush between the bowl and seat, with the brush hovering over the bowl. Spray brush with vinegar or antibacterial cleaner and air-dry before placing back in the dry toilet brush holder.

- Clean the floor (see pages 116–9).

Stained toilet

- Put on a pair of rubber gloves and apply Bar Keepers Friend Toilet Bowl Cleaner generously to the inside of the toilet bowl, starting at the rim, down the sides of the bowl and in the drain hole.

- Let it soak for at least 5 minutes. Do not close the toilet lid.

- Scrub the entire bowl thoroughly with a toilet brush, particularly where the staining is, then flush.

- You may need to repeat this process to remove some remnants of staining.
- Flush toilet, placing toilet brush in the running water to rinse thoroughly.

Strong odour

- Some toilet seats can be removed from the hinge, which allows you to give a deeper clean. If you find a stinky build-up under this hidden area, apply Lemon Soda Paste.
- Dab the paste onto the area and around the base of the toilet where it meets the floor. Leave to sit for 10 minutes.
- Spray vinegar over the paste and sit for a further 5 minutes.
- Remove build-up with paper towel.
- Finish by wiping over with cleaning spray using a paper towel.

HOW OFTEN?

Weekly.

THE TOOTHBRUSH HOLDER

Toothbrush holders can get very grimy, especially those cups you may not look into. After brushing your teeth, the wet toothbrush is placed back in the holder; the water drips down the handle, collecting in the base. The result can be quite a horrifying sight if the holder has not been cleaned in a while. I like to use a wall-mounted toothbrush holder, as it reduces benchtop clutter and keeps toothbrushes cleaner.

KIT

Cleaning cloths

Dishwashing liquid

Mini cleaning brush

White vinegar

STEPS

- Remove toothbrushes and wipe over with a cloth. Fill a cup with vinegar and add the toothbrushes, bristle end up.

- Soak the holder in hot water for 10 minutes and rinse.

- Fill the sink with warm soapy water, use a cleaning cloth or mini brush to clean all parts of the toothbrush holder, inside and out. Rinse.

- Fill or spray the toothbrush holder with vinegar and leave to sit for 5 minutes.

- Empty, rinse and dry with a dry cleaning cloth. Return toothbrush to the holder.

HOW OFTEN?

Weekly.

TV AND COMPUTER SCREENS

Flatscreen televisions and computer screens are sensitive and can be easily scratched and damaged during cleaning. Be very gentle while cleaning as pushing and scrubbing the screen may cause pixels to burn out. Using chemicals, window cleaner, soap or abrasive powder on the TV or computer screen may damage or discolour the screen. Check your manual for instructions to ensure that you do not clean it in a manner that will void your warranty.

KIT

Cleaning cloths

Kat's Sparkle Spray (see page 58)

Do not use rags, tissues, paper towels or toilet paper as these may scratch the screen.

STEPS

- Turn off the television or computer and unplug the power cord. This will make it easier to see the fingerprints and dust.

- Use a dry clean cleaning cloth to gently wipe the screen and frame.

- If needed to remove stubborn marks, lightly dampen a clean cloth with cleaner. Do not spray the solution directly onto the screen as this may damage the screen. Gently wipe over the screen.

- Let the screen dry completely, then plug the TV back in.

HOW OFTEN?
Weekly.

UPHOLSTERY

Leaving dirt on your couch will wear away the fibres, making your lounge look drab. Always check manufacturer's care instructions. Test a small area at the back of the couch for discolouration before proceeding. As with any spot cleans, it is best to clean the stain as soon as it's happened, as leaving it too long may allow the stain to set and become harder to remove. I like to deep clean my couch in the evening so it dries while we are sleeping.

KIT

Vacuum cleaner with upholstery and crevice attachment

Duster

Cleaning cloths

Kat's Cleaning Spray (see page 57) or fabric upholstery cleaner

Bicarb soda

Silicone glove, for pet hair

Leather cleaner

Make sure you use a similar-coloured cleaning cloth to your couch, ensuring the colour of the cloth does not transfer to the lounge.

STEPS

Quick clean

- Vacuum the couch with the upholstery attachment. If the cushions are detachable, vacuum both sides. Change to a crevice tool and get into the seams and crevices to pick up all dirt and food crumbs.

- Use a duster, or spray cleaning spray onto a cleaning cloth and wipe any wood or metal pieces such as the legs to remove dust build-up.

- For any smells, sprinkle bicarb soda over the couch, let sit for 30 minutes then vacuum. Remember to empty and clean your vacuum.

- For pet hair, a silicone glove works wonders. By running the glove over the surface, the friction between the glove and the fabric creates static energy, picking up pet hair with the bristles.

Spot clean

- Lightly spray with Kat's Cleaning Spray or fabric upholstery cleaner, dabbing with a cleaning cloth until the stain lifts. Do not rub the fabric. Dab the area with a slightly damp cloth dipped in warm water to pick up any soapy residue. Use another dry cloth, again dabbing at the area repeatedly to lift as much water as possible. Do not leave the area too damp as this may cause a water stain. Allow the area to dry thoroughly before use.

- For leather, spray with leather cleaner and wipe over with a cloth.

- For grease stains on fabric, sprinkle the area with bicarb soda, then sit for 30 minutes to soak up the grease. Vacuum area. Dab with a dry cleaning cloth to pick up any remaining grease. Clean vacuum.

Deep clean

- Carpet cleaning machines can be used on fabric lounges to pick up lingering dirt, sweat and odours sitting in the fabric fibres. These machines are available for hire from large hardware stores or supermarkets. Alternatively, there are some small hand-held spot-clean machines available at department stores. It is important to remember not to use too much water to prevent water stains on your upholstery.

- Follow the manufacturer's instructions to clean your upholstery. Keep the air in the room circulating (turn the fan on if you have one) while drying. I deep clean in the evening so the fabric dries while we are sleeping.

- Do not sit on the couch until it is completely dry.

HOW OFTEN?
Immediately – spot clean.
Weekly – quick and spot clean.
Seasonally – deep clean.

THE VACUUM CLEANER

A clean and well-maintained vacuum cleaner will do a much more efficient job of sucking up dust and dirt around your home. It will also last longer. Typically, if your machine is having suction problems, the filters and bag may need attention. Not emptying the dust and dirt from your vacuum regularly will cause it to smell (which will spread through the home while vacuuming) and become a breeding ground for mould and germs.

Before cleaning your vacuum, please read the manual for instructions on how to replace the filters and which parts are safe to wash.

KIT

Dishwashing liquid

Mini cleaning brush

Scissors

Broom

Kat's Cleaning Spray (see page 57) or multi-purpose cleaner

Cleaning cloth

STEPS

After each use

- Bagless vacuum: empty canister. After every few uses, empty and wash the canister in warm soapy water and completely air-dry.

- Vacuum with bag: check the indicator light; if full, replace the bag.

To clean the filter

- Remove the filter from the vacuum and use a mini brush to dislodge dust and hair.

- If the filter is washable, wash with warm water, gently rubbing away dirt build-up with your hands. Shake filter to remove excess water.

- Allow to air-dry completely before placing back in the vacuum.

To clean the brush heads

- Remove the head from the vacuum. You may find that the roller can easily be removed.

- Use a mini brush to help remove all hair, dust and dirt from the roller and head. For any hair tangled around the roller carefully cut – don't pull – using scissors, taking care not to cut any bristles.

- If the roller is removable and washable, wash it with warm water and dishwashing liquid, cleaning away any leftover dust and hair from the bristles. Completely air-dry before placing back in the head.

- Check the opening of the head for any blockages or dust clumps and clean away with the mini brush and a cloth.

To unblock the vacuum hose

- Switch off and unplug the vacuum cleaner.

- Undo the hose and check the entrance to the machine for clumps of dust and hair.

- Check each end of the hose for visible blockages.

- Carefully push a broom handle through the hose to help dislodge the blockage.

To clean the exterior

- Lightly spray cleaner onto a cloth and wipe over the inside and outside of the vacuum to remove any dust and dirt.

HOW OFTEN?
Monthly.

WALLS

Children or pets running in the home are guaranteed to result in dirty walls and scuff marks. Dust may also settle when windows are left open. It's important to not use too much soap on the walls as the residue is hard to remove and will attract dirt and dust.

KIT

Duster

Melamine foam or cleaning paste

Cleaning cloths

Tea tree or eucalyptus essential oil

Paper towel

Kat's Cleaning Spray (see page 57), multi-purpose cleaner or Kat's Reusable Wipes (see page 58)

STEPS

- Use a duster to remove any dust from the walls.

- For stubborn marks, use the melamine foam; alternatively use cleaning paste with a cleaning cloth, dabbing onto the wall and gently wiping to remove the mark. Wipe away cleaning paste with cleaning spray and a cloth.

- For sticky marks, use a few drops of tea tree or eucalyptus essential oil on a cleaning cloth or paper towel, wipe on the area and allow to sit for 5 minutes. Wipe away the sticky residue.

- Lightly spray cleaner on the wall and wipe your way from top to bottom, left to right. Alternatively, use wipes to clean.

HOW OFTEN?
Seasonally.

Kat's tip

To remove grease from walls
(in the kitchen around your
rangehood), a little lemon
juice works wonders. The acidic
properties assist in cutting through
grease and grime. Simply add the
juice from 1 lemon to your Kat's
Cleaning Spray and clean away.

THE WASHING MACHINE

Have you ever washed your washing machine? Sounds funny but it collects a lot of dust, dirt and grime, so it needs a regular clean to ensure your clothes smell fresh. Front loader washing machines are also well known for the build-up of mould around the seal; a musty smell could be your first indication that this is occurring. It's very important to clean away mould and soap build-up as it can transfer to your clothes during the washing cycle and become harmful to your health.

Please check your manual for instructions for your particular machine and make sure the washing machine is empty with no clothes inside before cleaning.

KIT

Kat's Washing Machine Spray (see page 59)

Paper towel

Gloves

Bleach

Kat's Cleaning Spray (see page 57) or antibacterial spray

White vinegar

Cleaning cloth

Dishwashing liquid

Cleaning paste or Lemon Soda Paste (see page 59)

Mini cleaning brush

Scrubbing brush

Dustpan and brush and broom, for behind the washing machine

Mop and bucket, for behind the washing machine

STEPS

Quick clean

- After each wash, spritz with Kat's Washing Machine Spray and leave the door or lid open for the machine to dry.

Deep clean

Front loader

- Check for mould. Pull back the seal with your fingers behind a paper towel (or wear gloves), spray bleach onto mould. Allow bleach to sit for 5 minutes, then wipe away with a paper towel. Spray seal with cleaning spray and wipe again with paper towel to remove all bleach remnants.

- Clean the drum. Pour 1–2 cups vinegar (depending on washer size) into the detergent dispenser, then run an empty hot temperature cycle.

- Clean seal. Spray the seal with cleaning spray and wipe away any grime build-up with a cloth. Give the seal a final spritz of washing machine spray. Leave door open to allow seal and drum to dry.

- Clean filter and soap/fabric dispenser. Remove the lint trap or drain pump filter and soap dispenser from the washing machine. Rinse under hot water to remove built-up gunk. Fill up the laundry sink with warm soapy water. Place filter and dispenser into the sink, use a mini brush to remove trapped particles. Rinse with clean water and let sit to air-dry before returning.

- Clean exterior. Spray the exterior with cleaning spray and cloth to remove any scuff marks. Use cleaning paste or Lemon Soda Paste for stubborn marks, wiping clean with a damp cloth.

Top loader

- Clean filter and soap/fabric dispenser. Remove the filter and dispenser from the washing machine. Rinse under hot water to remove built-up gunk. Fill up the laundry sink with warm soapy water. Place filter and dispenser into the sink, use a mini brush to remove trapped particles. Rinse with clean water and let sit to air-dry before returning.

- While empty, put the washing machine through a hot temperature full cycle. Add 1 cup vinegar as it fills.

- As the machine is filling up, use the water and a cloth to wipe:

    Top of the washer

    Lid

    Outside the washer

    Underneath the lid

    Rim of the washing machine

    Top of the spinner

    Filter location

    All nooks and crannies you can find dirt and dust build-up.

- If grime build-up in your washing machine does not disappear in this cleaning cycle, use a scrubbing brush to brush away all the soap build-up and repeat with another empty wash.

Behind the washing machine

- Unplug your machine and carefully pull it away from the wall.

- Using your dustpan brush or a dry cleaning cloth, wipe away any dust sitting on the electrical cord and on the back of the machine. If dust is stuck on, carefully use the brush attachment on your vacuum cleaner to remove it.

- Use a broom and dustpan to sweep up the dust and dirt under the machine. Alternatively, you could use your vacuum, but more than likely it could be sticky and you don't really want that in your vacuum. Mop the floor.

- Once the floor is dry, move the washing machine back into place and plug it back in.

HOW OFTEN?

Daily – quick clean.

Weekly – clean front loader seal.

Monthly – deep clean.

Seasonally – clean behind the machine.

How to prevent mould in your machine

Front loader washing machines are renowned for developing mould and bacteria very easily. After use, the machine is normally still very damp. An excess of moisture and a build-up of soap scum in a closed machine is the perfect breeding ground for mould growth. Follow my quick tips below every time you use your machine to prevent your front loader from getting mouldy.

1. Do not leave wet clothes to sit in the machine – remove wet clothes promptly.

2. After use, wipe down the seal and door to remove any moisture – I keep a microfibre cloth handy for this.

3. Leave the door open. I keep the cloth in the door to prevent it from closing. (I have a habit of closing the door if I see it open, but the cloth reminds me to open it to dry.)

4. Spray regularly with Kat's Washing Machine Spray (see page 59).

Kat's tip

Did you know you can use white vinegar instead of fabric softener in the wash? Vinegar acts as a natural disinfectant, killing germs, bacteria or mould present in the linens and removes soap residue. It won't make the clothes smell like vinegar and the bonus is it's so cheap and will soften your clothes! Please check your manual to see if vinegar can be used in your washing machine.

WINDOWS

Cleaning windows is one of the tasks that I regularly neglected when the kids were younger. It was a hopeless cause to have sparkling clean windows when there were curious little fingers around. However, when windows are clean, they look so good – and I love allowing the sunshine to beam in through the glass. Dirty windows can be unsightly, plus the build-up can leave scratches on your glass.

Dust and dirt settles in the window tracks and sills so it's important to clean this away first to avoid a muddy mess. Most window cleaning solutions should leave a quick-drying streak-free shine, eliminating the need to use the old squeegee. Microfibre cloths are a great lint-free and super-absorbent option.

It's best to clean your windows early in the morning or on a cloudy day as heat can speed up the drying process and leave smears. If your window is hot to touch, wait for a cooler day or start on the shady side of the house. And if you can't reach all your windows, get in the professionals!

KIT

Kat's Sparkle Spray (see page 58) or glass cleaner

Microfibre cloths

Scrubbing brush

Dishwashing liquid

Window-track cleaning brush

Mini cleaning brush

Vacuum cleaner with crevice attachment

Kat's Cleaning Spray (see page 57) or multi-purpose cleaner

When you're cleaning, wipe the internal side of the window horizontally and the external vertically. If a streak appears, you'll easily know which side it is on.

STEPS

Spot clean

- Spritz glass cleaner onto glass. Use a clean dry cleaning cloth to spot clean.

Quick clean

- Spray window with glass cleaner. Starting from the top and working your way down, use a clean dry cleaning cloth to clean the internal window.

Deep clean

- Remove any screen (if you can). Clean screen with a scrubbing brush and warm soapy water on a hard-surfaced area or in the bathtub lined with a towel to prevent scratches (not on the lawn as this will make a muddy mess). Rinse with water and air-dry.
- Use the window-track cleaning brush to loosen up any dirt build-up in the window tracks. Use the mini brush to get into hard-to-reach corners.
- Use the vacuum crevice tool to pick up all the dirt in the tracks and windowsill.
- Spray window with cleaning spray. Starting from the top and working your way down, use a microfibre cloth to wipe away dirt or cobwebs from window.
- Wipe over the window frame and track again to remove any drips from cleaning.
- Wipe windowsill with cloth and cleaning spray.

- To make your windows shine, spritz glass cleaner onto glass. Use a clean dry cleaning cloth to clean internal and external window.

- Place dry screen back onto window.

HOW OFTEN?

You may need to deep clean seasonally if you live in an area with dust stirring regularly outside.

Weekly – spot clean (kitchen and living area).
Monthly – quick clean.
Seasonally – window tracks.
Annually – deep clean.

Make deep cleaning windows easier by tackling it room by room over the course of the year.

ACKNOWLEDGEMENTS

Firstly, thank you to my dad, mum, nan and nanna, who have played a special part in making me the person I am today.

To the incredible team at Pan Macmillan, thank you. Cate Blake, for encouraging me to write this book. Rebecca Lay, Ariane Durkin and Mark Thacker, for making it happen and for all you do.

My thanks to Kate, Alex and Danielle for your words of wisdom and subtle nudges in helping me realise that I can write a book. It's a wonder what you can achieve with a bit of focus.

Thank you to my very talented photographer, Kaitlin Rees, for her amazing ability to interpret what I want a photo to express and delivering them ever so beautifully.

For their gracious support – enormous appreciation to my team at Organised HQ. Thank you for all you have done towards the success of The Organised Housewife and Organised HQ, for motivating me to make this book a reality, and for making it possible for me to get offline and write.

I have endless gratitude to my incredible husband, Scott – for saying yes to dancing with me at our high school formal, being by my side through tears and triumphs, and always making me feel beautiful. Thank you for supporting and encouraging me and making every day brighter.

To my kids, Joshua, Isabella and Haylee – I'm tremendously proud of each of you. Thank you for the love you give me, the heart you have filled and for putting up with the craziness and time out I needed to write this book.

Thank you to my mother-in-law, Lynda – little does she know the impact she has made on the mother I am today. She has the biggest heart and has always been there when I need her.

My brothers Michael and Steven and brother-in-law Brett – I'm so thankful to have you all in my life and appreciate your constant care and always asking, 'How are you?' or 'How is work?'

A special thank you to my best friends, Sarah, Sandy, Anneliese and Cathy, who have always been my cheerleaders and believers.

Thank you to The Organised Housewife community, who continue to inspire me to keep sharing the realities of everyday life.

And finally to you, lovely reader, this book is for you. I hope it motivates, encourages and inspires you to make your home exactly how you want it to feel.

Kat xxx

Remember my motto:

Imperfectly perfect is good enough.

INDEX

THE ORGANISED HOUSEWIFE

theorganisedhousewife.com.au

The Organised Housewife blog is where Kat's journey of sharing her tips and ideas for creating calm in the home began. You can find a wide range of articles – with new ones published each week – covering a range of topics from cleaning and organising, to recipes, weekly meal plans and much more!

organisedHQ

organisedhq.com.au

Organised HQ is an online store selling a wide selection of organising, cleaning, home and living products, covering all areas of the home. Starting Organised HQ was a long-held dream of Kat's, particularly as her readers would always seek advice on what cleaning and organising products she could recommend. Everything is personally sourced, tried and tested so that Organised HQ can be your trusted go-to store for must-have products.

Get 10% off* use coupon code CLEANHOME10 at checkout.

*discount excludes sale items, valid for one transaction.

Pan Macmillan acknowledges the Traditional Custodians of Country throughout Australia and their connections to lands, waters and communities. We pay our respect to Elders past and present and extend that respect to all Aboriginal and Torres Strait Islander peoples today. We honour more than sixty thousand years of storytelling, art and culture.

First published 2022 in Macmillan by Pan Macmillan Australia Pty Limited
Level 25, 1 Market Street, Sydney, New South Wales Australia 2000

 A catalogue record for this book is available from the National Library of Australia

Design by Mark Thacker

Proofread by Megan Johnston

Index by Helena Holmgren

Colour + reproduction by Splitting Image Colour Studio

Printed in China by Imago

10 9 8 7 6 5 4 3 2 1